MW01452271

Praise for
SHOVELING $H!T

"An unflinching look at what it really takes to succeed. Kass and Mike dive into the crap every entrepreneur has to deal with while building a business and emerge with hard-won lessons about starting, managing, pivoting—and learning to love the shovel along the way."

    SCOTT GALLOWAY, Professor at NYU Stern School of Business, Host of *Prof G Pod* and Co-Host of the *Pivot* Podcast

"Mike and Kass is the greatest partnership I've ever been lucky enough to witness in person. Not just in business but in life, they bring out the best in each other and all of those around them. This book is a wonderful map to success both personal and professional from two of the most special people I know."

    SETH MEYERS, Host of *Late Night with Seth Meyers*

"Being an entrepreneur is messy, gritty, and often far from glamorous—and *Shoveling $h!t* tells it like it is. Kass and Mike offer an unfiltered look at the inevitable struggles every entrepreneur faces while building a successful business from the ground up. No-nonsense and straight-talking, *Shoveling $h!t* is the business book of the future."

    MEL ROBBINS, Bestselling Author and Host of *The Mel Robbins Podcast*

amplify
an imprint of Amplify Publishing Group

www.amplifypublishinggroup.com

Shoveling $h!t: A Love Story About the Entrepreneur's Messy Path to Success

©2025 Michael & Kass Lazerow. All Rights Reserved. No part of this publication may be reproduced, stored in a retrieval system or transmitted in any form by any means electronic, mechanical, or photocopying, recording or otherwise without the permission of the author.

The views and opinions expressed in this book are solely those of the authors and do not necessarily represent those of the publisher or staff. The publisher assumes no responsibility for errors, inaccuracies, omissions, or any other inconsistencies herein.

For more information, please contact:
Amplify Publishing, an imprint of Amplify Publishing Group
620 Herndon Parkway, Suite 220
Herndon, VA 20170
info@amplifypublishing.com

Library of Congress Control Number: 2024919627

CPSIA Code: PRV0225A

ISBN-13: 979-8-89138-351-7

Printed in the United States

To our kids—Myles, Cole, and Vivian—who endured our absences and bore the brunt of our crap as entrepreneurs. Being your parents has been the greatest experience of our lives by far and we are proud of the people you are. We love you always.

SHOVELING
$H!T

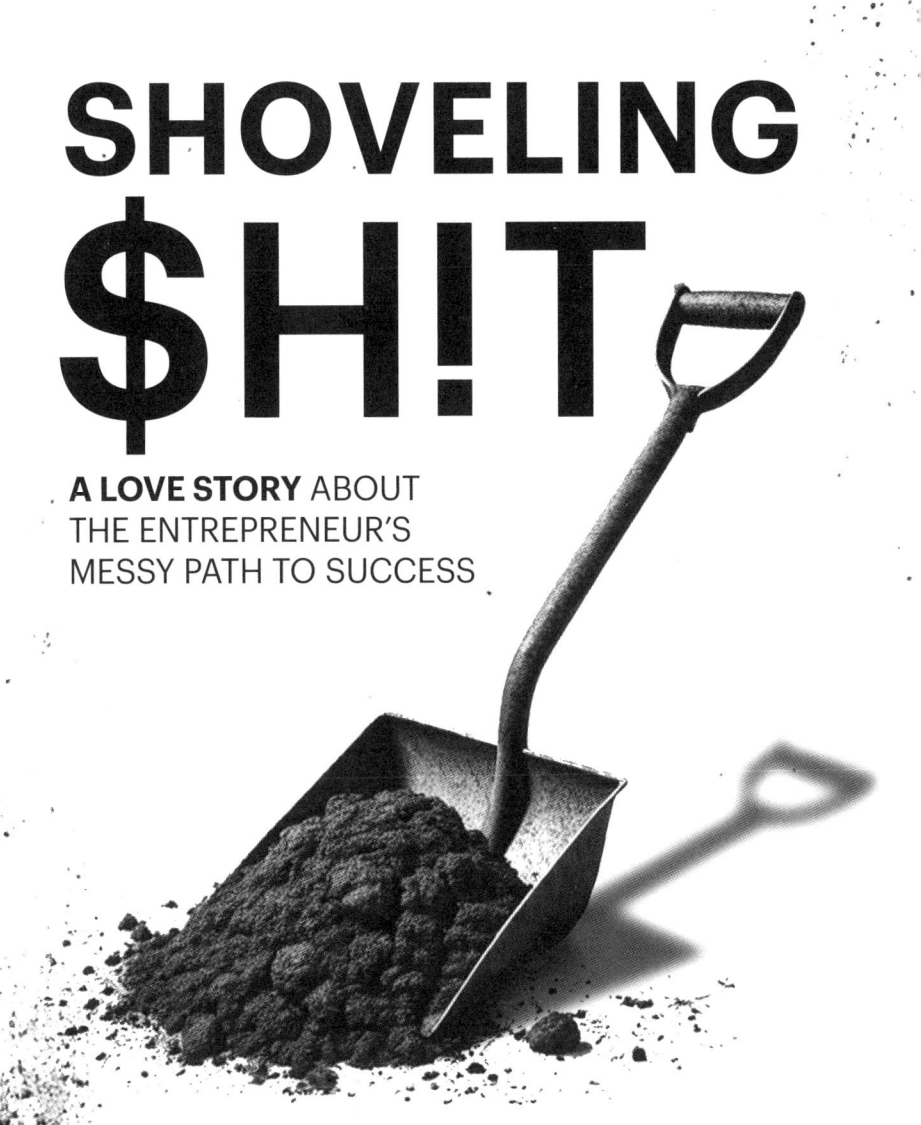

A LOVE STORY ABOUT
THE ENTREPRENEUR'S
MESSY PATH TO SUCCESS

Kass and Mike Lazerow

amplify
an imprint of Amplify Publishing Group

CONTENTS

FOREWORD — 1
BY GARY VAYNERCHUK

BEFORE YOU SHOVEL THIS CRAP — 5

THE DAY IT HIT THE FAN — 11
WANT TO BE AN ENTREPRENEUR? GET READY FOR SOME CRAP.

ENTREPRENEURIAL ORIGINS — 25
THE CRAP WE'RE BORN INTO IS THE CRAP FROM WHICH WE GROW.

THE IMBALANCED LIFE — 43
THE CRAP THAT COMES WITH THE PRESSURES ON YOUR PERSONAL LIFE.

SAYING "I DO" — 61
PICKING THE RIGHT PARTNERS IS ESSENTIAL FOR DEALING WITH THE CRAP THAT'S COMING YOUR WAY.

CHECKING THE GO GAUGE — 77
THE CRAP THAT COMES WITH VETTING THE IDEA.

FEEDING THE BABY — 95
THE CRAP THAT COMES WITH FUNDING THE BUSINESS.

SITTING AND SHOVELING — 113
HYPER-FOCUSING ON THE RIGHT CRAP ONCE YOU START THE BUSINESS.

MONEYBALLING YOUR TEAM — 127
THE CRAP THAT COMES WITH HIRING FAST AND FIRING FASTER.

PUTTING THE CULT IN YOUR CULTURE 147
THE SHOVELING THAT COMES WITH CREATING
A CRAP-FREE CULTURE.

LEADERS SHOVEL FIRST 165
THE CRAP THAT COMES WITH LEADING A STARTUP.

PERCEPTION IS REALITY 179
THE CRAP THAT COMES WITH MARKETING
FOR SUCCESS.

DEATH AND THE PIVOT 195
THE ENTREPRENEUR'S ULTIMATE CRAP-SHOVELING
EXERCISE.

EXIT 209
THE FLOWERS THAT COME FROM LOVING THE SHOVEL.

ACKNOWLEDGMENTS 223
ABOUT THE AUTHORS 229

FOREWORD

BY GARY VAYNERCHUK

When Kass and Mike shared their book with me, I immediately offered my full and unconditional support to help make it a bestseller.

Why would I do that?

It's not just that they are two of my favorite people, which they are. Or that they opened their hearts and their office to me when I needed it, which they did. The reason is simple: the world needs to be exposed to Kass and Mike—how they think, how they operate businesses, how they give back, how they parent, and how they treat everyone in their lives.

I met Kass and Mike in 2009. I had just left my family business to start VaynerMedia with my brother AJ. Even though I had a cult following from years of doing Wine Library TV and building a massive business for my father, I never really made that much money in a single year. I was just like many of the readers—high on ideas, confidence, and energy, and low on financial resources to start building.

I needed an office for our small team—myself, AJ, and four of his friends, all working for free. I asked Mike, and later Kass, as I now know she runs the show, to take over their conference room in their office near New York's Columbus Circle for the very first VaynerMedia office. This was a colossal and unreasonable ask. Buddy Media was a tiny startup with limited resources, and I didn't ask to take over its only conference room for a meeting or a day. I asked to move in indefinitely until we had the money to get our office, locking them out of their only meeting room. (In fact, I didn't ask, Mike offered because that's just who he is.)

Not only did they offer me the space but they treated us like family, offering us their food, drinks, and ping pong table.

So, when Kass and Mike told me about this project and the title, *Shoveling $h!t,* I knew I had to get involved.

I now employ more than two thousand people across my family of companies. While I no longer share office space with Kass and Mike, we are great friends who continue to work, invest, and give back together.

They were among my first calls when I was thinking about launching Empathy Wines. They said yes immediately. When I decided to raise money for Veefriends, they were two of the people I called right away, and they said yes immediately. When I wanted value-added co-owners for my pickleball team, the New Jersey 5s, guess who I called? They said yes right away.

In return, I just hope to say yes whenever a call is made.

With this book, you too can lean on them and the 50+ lessons they share—lessons learned and earned the hard way, struggling through business and life.

Every company is different. The entrepreneurial mindset is not. Nor are the lessons Kass and Mike share about their biggest successes and most painful failures. Any entrepreneur who doesn't run fast to read this book is grossly negligent.

Most people want cheat codes, easy money, and shortcuts. If you are a fan of mine, you know the truth—there are no shortcuts, just hard work. Behind every "overnight success" are years and years and years of hard, and often painful work. And that is precisely what this book is about—it is Kass and Mike's brutally honest love letter to the hard work they put in over almost three decades to generate the mind-blowing success you see today while raising three awesome kids I adore.

Kass and Mike's story is my story, and the story of every entrepreneur who bets on themselves, hustles, and turns hard work into entrepreneurial riches. It can be your story, too, if you decide to pick up a shovel.

What are you waiting for? Dig in!

Gary

Gary is a serial entrepreneur who serves as the chairman of VaynerX, the CEO of VaynerMedia, and the creator and CEO of VeeFriends.

BEFORE YOU SHOVEL THIS CRAP

Entrepreneurship is booming. Nearly one in five adults around the world are in the process of founding a business or have done so in the past three and a half years.[*] The bold and the brave launched a record five and a half million new businesses in 2023.[†] And it's a safe bet that many more thought of starting a business but never did.

If you spend your days working for someone else, chances are that you have fantasized about starting a company. You know the dream. Will you make it your reality?

The allure of starting a business is strong and can blind the senses. There's the promise of freedom. Entrepreneurs can do what they want, when they want, as they want, right? Then there's the

---

[*] "Global Entrepreneurship Monitor 2022-2023," *Global Entrepreneurship Monitor,* August 22, 2023, https://issuu.com/babsoncollege/docs/brndrep4-279 5-gem-2023-final-pages.

[†] "How Many New Businesses Are Started Each Year? 2024 Data Reveals the Answer." *Commerce Institute,* accessed August 7, 2024. https://www.commerceinstitute.com/new-businesses-started-every-year/.

payoff—the big pot of gold at the end of the entrepreneurial rainbow. Success stories pervade the media—examples of people who took an idea, turned it into a business, sold it for a bazillion dollars, and jetted off to an early retirement. The proliferation of social media has only intensified the feeling that everyone is starting businesses and succeeding.

There's just one problem with that narrative: like much of the crap that spreads far and wide online, it's not true.

Well, it's mostly untrue. There is (some) freedom, provided your definition includes shoveling a bottomless pit of crap. And a payoff is possible, it's just not guaranteed. But regardless of the financial outcome, you can count on immense pressure, hard work, difficult decisions and conversations, stress, and failures—not to mention sacrifices and more sacrifices and even more sacrifices. You can count on some crap.

A family member who invested threatens to sue. Someone quits, gets sick, or has a family emergency when you are in the middle of a game-changing moment. Markets crash weeks before your next round of fundraising. Customers cancel or go out of business. Banks fail. Shareholders are added to the government sanctions list and funds are frozen. Pandemics, hurricanes, and terrorists cripple domestic travel. Your original business idea is languishing and you have to pivot.

We have lived through all of that in our careers, and you will experience similar tribulations if you do it long enough.

We've been involved as founders in three high-growth startups, two of them working as a couple. U-Wire and Golf.com both sold for a small profit, but we're most often associated with Buddy Media, which we cofounded in 2007 and grew into the world's leading social media marketing platform, then later sold to Salesforce in 2012 for $745 million.

Since Buddy Media, we've created an operating company and have been active as investors for hundreds of startups, not to mention advisors to many more. We've been involved in some companies that have done extremely well and became household names, like Facebook, Scopely, Liquid Death, and Tumblr. Others failed miserably, leaving crap on our faces and our family's balance sheet lighter.

While not all of our ventures turned manure into roses, we have started or been seed investors in startups that have generated more than $10 billion in realized gains for investors. And we've learned from every company along the way. But to be crystal clear, none of these companies have been simply "up and to the right." All have had their oh-shit moments, and that's why we're writing this book. The life of an entrepreneur isn't for everyone, but we believe everyone chasing a dream can benefit from our entrepreneurial love story.

That's right. We consider this book—a book about shoveling entrepreneurial crap—an epic love story. And not because we're married, although we do love each other. But we've come to believe a key ingredient in any entrepreneur's success is a love for shoveling the shit that comes with the work.

Our romance with entrepreneurship has been driven by an emotional investment so deep that our work often became an extension of our very being. The arduous path of building a company and not just a career is a profound affair of the heart—even if it's at times smelly and messy.

We didn't set out to write a comprehensive "how-to" book. Nor was our goal to write the "best" book ever on entrepreneurship.

Our aim was quite simple—to create one of the most honest books you'll ever read about starting and growing a business. That means we won't just write about the *idea* of loving the entrepreneurial life, we write about the very real crap that comes with it.

While most of the stories in this book are unique to us, the lessons are universal—lessons we wish we would have known before starting any of our companies. So we believe *Shoveling $h!t* will help you avoid mistakes and minimize how much crap you get on yourself and the people around you. More importantly, it will prepare you to deal with the messes you can't avoid no matter how perfectly you plan, how well you execute, or how closely you follow the best advice.

And, as we discovered while reliving our biggest challenges and mistakes, we think you'll find that not all manure is bad, regardless of how bad it smells and how much time and pain it takes to shovel away. Just as some cultures use it to heat ovens, crap can fuel the entrepreneurial flame. And just as good farmers spread it on their crops, entrepreneurs can learn to harness it to fertilize their field of dreams.

We love entrepreneurs and have proactively surrounded ourselves with them. We also know how hard it is to build companies. If you want to succeed as a founder, learn to love shoveling crap because it's the only way to ensure your fledgling company doesn't drown in it, or better yet, learn to create fertilizer that helps grow something amazing.

And by amazing, we don't just mean profitable, although that's vital. No profits, no business. We mean amazing by the modern standards of capitalism, which is to say the company makes a profit, adds value to stakeholders, and serves the greater good, or at least a greater need, in the world around it.

Is that too much to ask?

We think not.

We wrote this book for current entrepreneurs of all ages and everyone who dreams of becoming one. We also wrote this book for the risk-taking investors who fund the dreams of the dreamers. Without our many investors, we would never have been able to grow our businesses. Investors who have not built businesses will never understand the pain and hard work of the entrepreneurial journey. But we hope this book gives them a view into the life of the entrepreneur—one that will help them bring more compassion and empathy as they help entrepreneurs turn their dreams into reality.

WHO'S DRIVING THIS BOOK, ANYWAY?

We have always tried to play to our strengths, whether it's in the companies we've started, the ventures we've supported, or the way we've managed our marriage and raised our children. This book is no different.

We each have unique skills and experiences. We work together, but we also do our own things. For instance, Mike has always been a trend-spotting idea-guy who is great at casting and selling a vision, while Kass has been the operational mastermind and the voice of reason.

As co-authors, we wanted to capture the magic that comes from a merging of our differences. We didn't want a book by Kass with Mike or by Mike with Kass. We wanted a book by Kass and Mike. Different people. Equal partners.

Most books are written with a single voice. We tried that, but it diluted the value of our partnership—not just as business partners but as partners in marriage since 1999. So, we wrote this book just like we have done everything else—together but as unique individuals. The result more accurately captures our journey. Any other approach and you would have missed out on the best of what we as a team have to offer—not just two voices but two perspectives presented in a really raw way that reflects how we communicate and work together.

So, while there's no question that we are co-authors, you will hear our stories and learn what we know from three perspectives: Mike's, Kass's, and ours. Mostly, we'll write in first person plural. *We did this . . . A few things occurred to us.* But that can get confusing in cases where one of us uniquely owns the experience and perspective that's coming from a story. So, if we drop into first person or third person, it's not an ego thing. We're just trying to be helpful and clear.

I (Mike) will be me when the story needs to be told by me. And I (Kass) will be me when the story is mine to tell.

Most of all, we think you'll appreciate and learn more from this unique way of sharing what we know. So, from each of us and from both of us, we/Mike/Kass hope you enjoy the journey into our entrepreneurial minds.

THE DAY IT HIT THE FAN

WANT TO BE AN ENTREPRENEUR? GET READY FOR SOME CRAP.

The phone call changed everything.

It was February 2000, and we were living the entrepreneurial dream. Our seedling idea of an online golf site had produced a flowering sprout that we considered pretty special.

Thanks to a good idea, hard work, and a young golfer named Tiger Woods, we had momentum. In 1999, the first full year that we had our site up and running, Tiger won eight tournaments, solidifying his status as the number one golfer on the planet. At just twenty-three years old, Tiger had become a global cultural icon who transcended his sport, creating what was aptly coined the "Tiger Effect."

Golf participation boomed—up 20 percent in the five years after Tiger turned pro. Television viewership spiked, with PGA Tour events regularly beating the hottest NBA matchups. The largest companies in the world lined up to associate with Tiger and his hot global brand—General Motors, EA Sports, American Express, Titleist, TLC Laser Eye, Rolex, and Nike doled out more than $50 million.

The excitement drove immense traffic to our startup golf venture which drew much of its revenue from Tiger's sponsors. Investors, partners, and potential suitors were now contacting us. After nearly two years of nonstop grinding, we leaned into an offer to merge with another hot company, Chipshot.com, in an all-stock deal to build a behemoth in the golf space.

Chipshot was planning an IPO when its competitors were raising hundreds of millions of dollars in their market debuts. Our budding little flower was about to be worth many times our initial investment.

Then a dump truck full of unexpected crap arrived in the form of a phone call, and there was nothing we could do but grab our shovels and start digging our way out.

TEEING OFF WITH ONLINE GOLF—KASS

Our company, which I launched as GolfServ Online in September of 1998, had a unique vertical at the very beginnings of the commercial internet—Web 1.0, as it's now known.

The concept originated in my very competitive heart. I was recruited to play tennis at Dartmouth, and I did so for almost two seasons before injuries took me out. At the urging of the golf coach and two of my closest college friends (Sarah Davis and Tracy Welch, both scratch golfers!) I joined them on the golf team during the fall semester of my senior year. That's when I learned the value of tracking my stats. After college, I kept tracking them using good ol' fashioned spreadsheets, the beginning of a lifelong love affair with rows and columns, pivot tables, and all things Excel (and now Google Sheets too).

I shared that spreadsheet with my father and closest-brother-in-age, James, and we added all our data: number of putts, fairways hit, greens hit in regulation, up-and-downs, etc. Out of the spreadsheet came rankings in different categories as well as an approximate handicap that took into account the different courses we all played. Bragging rights matter in our ultra-competitive family.

In the spring of 1998, the rankings weren't going to my liking and I voiced my displeasure to Mike. I was convinced that James was changing the stats. I didn't know how, but I was in last place in fairways hit, which was by far my best shot. Angry, I snapped to Mike, "This is such bullshit. I wish there were some way we could use the internet to enter all of our data into some sort of locked interface so that no one could manipulate their stats!"

In typical Mike fashion, a lightbulb went off. A very bright lightbulb. He turned to me and said, "Wait, I think we could do that." Then he paused and said, "And potentially more. Maybe we could even offer official handicaps online, especially to recreational golfers like us, and syndicate this content to a ton of sites! You might be onto something."

Mike and I were dating at the time and he was still running U-Wire, the company he started in 1993 as a student at Northwestern. U-Wire gathered articles from student newspapers around the country, compiled them, and then sent them out to those newspapers to use as supplements to their in-house copy. It was like a college version of the Associated Press. Rather than charging the newspapers, U-Wire locked down the commercial rights to their content and made money syndicating that content to professional news outlets and by sending press releases to the editors of the campus newspapers that companies wanted desperately to reach. Mike thought syndicating golf content seemed like a great opportunity as well.

So, I quit my marketing and business development job with GiantStep, a digital marketing agency spun out of legendary Chicago ad agency Leo Burnett, and founded the new company. I then convinced Mike Caspar—a close (and brilliant) friend who had also moved to Chicago from the DC area and was working at GiantStep—to join me. Mike came on board as the third partner after his company, U-Wire, merged with Student Advantage (a card-based membership program that provided students deep discounts for national and local companies) and went public on the NASDAQ stock exchange at the height of the dot-com craze.

With me as the operator, Caspar as the technical wizard, and Mike as the product-and-sales brain, we developed an internet-based software that empowered golfers with the tools to track and analyze their statistics. The software, which we sold to other websites, also provided leaderboards, online handicaps (to the USGA's chagrin), and live coverage of professional golf.

As early users of the internet were moving beyond general interest search engines like Yahoo!, Excite, and Looksmart, so too was our vision moving to eventually launch syndicated solutions in other verticals like travel, wellness, and food and wine that appealed to people with high-discretionary income.

Things were pretty much going to plan . . . until Chipshot.com entered the picture.

Chipshot.com was a Silicon Valley startup with an online store that sold custom knock-off golf clubs at a fraction of the price of large manufacturers like Titleist, Callaway, and TaylorMade. Amar Goel had started Chipshot.com as a nineteen-year-old student at Harvard with his brother Rajeev and good friend Nick Mehta. They had grown it to around $30 million in annual sales, making it one of the fastest-growing vertical e-commerce sites in the short history of the internet, and were looking to expand into media and other golf services.

With a vision grander than equipment, Chipshot.com approached us in June 1999—less than a year after we started the company—with an offer to buy GolfServ. On December 23, 1999, we closed an all-stock deal to merge the companies.

Happy Holidays, right?!

Newly married, we celebrated like it was 1999 (which it was) and threw a big Y2K bash at a favorite neighborhood restaurant, Blossom, in Chicago's Bucktown neighborhood. I (Kass) love to give raffle prizes and customized awards at our parties, so I brought a bounty of Chipshot.com golf products. The grand prize—a full set of Chipshot.com, TaylorMade knockoffs—went to Rob Janas, a Second City comedian and writer who, we are told, still plays with the clubs.

The deal seemed like a merger made in fairway heaven.

The company's pedigree was quintessential Silicon Valley—young Ivy League founder, funding from legendary venture capital firm Sequoia Capital, and a grow-by-all-means-necessary ethos. Sequoia's lead partner on the deal was Don Valentine, the firm's founder who made Sequoia's initial investment ($150,000) into Apple Inc. after meeting Steve Jobs back when Jobs was an engineer at Sequoia's very first investment, Atari. You may have heard of Sequoia's other early investments—Oracle Corp., Cisco, Electronic Arts, YouTube, and the little company that bought it, Google.

With Sequoia's backing, Chipshot.com's IPO was in the works for early 2000. Sure, our roles would change with new ownership. But this merger would allow us to take the company much further and work with like-minded innovators in a bigger market than just online golf media. The Chipshot.com founders told a powerful story, and you can't blame us or our board for buying it hook, line, and sinker.

The Chipshot.com deal closed just as the world reached peak internet euphoria. Investors were clamoring for all things internet.

The same month we started our discussions with Chipshot.com, a tiny company that sold toys through the internet called eToys.com raised about $166 million in a well-publicized public offering. The IPO was priced at twenty dollars per share, and on its first day of trading, the stock price skyrocketed, reaching a high of around seventy-six dollars and giving the young company a market valuation of about $7.7 billion. To put this in context, eToys was worth more than Apple at the time on the day eToys went public.

This wasn't an isolated story. In 1999, 298 IPOs raised $24.66 billion, up from $1.96 billion from 42 IPOs in 1998. Internet-related companies represented 60 percent of all IPOs in 1999, compared to 14 percent in 1998, and, like eToys, were embraced enthusiastically by investors. The average internet company's stock closed up 90 percent on the first day of trading and ended the year 266 percent above its offering price.[*]

---

[*] Westenberg, David. "Internet IPOs Conclude Sensational Year in 1999." *WilmerHale,* January 2000. https://www.wilmerhale.com/insights/publications/internet-ipos-conclude-sensational-year-in-1999-january-2000.

Chipshot.com and eToys were cut from the same cloth (or so we thought); both sold commodity products at discount prices to a global market of buyers through the internet. If eToys could go public and be valued more than Apple, why couldn't we? For a couple of young entrepreneurs from the East Coast, the prospect of being part of a Sequoia-backed rocket ship was too tantalizing to turn down. We were drunk on the excitement. Up and to the right was all we knew!

THE CALL

Back in the GolfServ office, the gap between dot-com Silicon Valley and industrial Chicago was immense. GolfServ's digs were sparse—a thousand or so square feet of office space across from a gas station and wedged between a furniture store and a Wendy's on the edge of Lincoln Park at the intersection of Fullerton and Clybourn Avenues. Behind the office ran a branch of the Chicago River that on a good day smelled like onions. Years and years of toxic runoff from chemical, food-processing, and steel companies made opening one of the few office windows a Category 1 health hazard.

Our "global headquarters," as we called it, was a one-bedroom apartment with two separate areas—the single bedroom and bathroom, and the open-floor-plan area that included the kitchen, dining, and living area. We shared an office with Caspar in the converted bedroom, and our employees were in the main area. Nothing was more cringe-worthy than being deep in discussion with customers or investors when other guests or employees exited the sole bathroom—the noise and smell wafting into the middle of our meeting.

It was in our shared office that we huddled around a speakerphone in February 2000 when Brian Sroub, the newly appointed

CEO of Chipshot.com, called with what we presumed was another update about the upcoming IPO.

It was an update, alright, just not the type we were expecting. Here's how we remember the call that kick-started our first hard lesson in paper profits versus hard cash.

Kass: "Hi Brian. How's it going?"

Brian: "Not good. Sequoia is out. Don no longer wants to back us."

Kass: "Wait, what?"

Brian: "Sequoia is out. Without new financing, we are done. And we no longer will be able to cover any of your payroll."

Mike: "Done?"

Brian: "Done as in done. Dead. Chipshot.com is going out of business without immediate funding."

He paused, and said, "But you can buy the company back if you want."

We sat stunned. *What the @#&%?!* Apparently, Sequoia's backing was never the done deal we were led to believe it was throughout our due diligence. And there was no Plan B.

We weren't worried about ourselves. When we merged with Chipshot.com, we were accustomed to no pay and making a whopping $30,000 each as founders. Our thoughts immediately turned to the dozen or so employees who relied on us, and to our investors, many of whom were family and close friends, whose money was now at real risk.

Welcome to the glamorous life of entrepreneurs. You know: Steve Jobs, Oprah Winfrey, Mark Zuckerberg, Arianna Huffington, Vera Wang, Mark Cuban, and us—Kass and Mike Lazerow.

Build it. Scale it. Sell it. Go public!

Rinse and repeat!

Champagne and caviar for everyone!

Until you get a phone call and learn you've just fallen from the top of the Sears Tower.

CHIPPING OUR WAY OUT OF A SANDCRAP

Most of the angel investors in GolfServ were our family members and close colleagues, so our first call after "the call" was to tell our angels their money had landed in the drink.

Roughly $1.5 million just went kerplunk, shank you very much.

And some of that money had come from the meager life savings of a young couple that had been married less than a few months—us.

One family member threatened to sue us, but we shrugged that off and devised a plan to shovel our way out of our mess.

We will never forget meeting with our employees the morning after Brian's call.

We had a history of transparency, so there was trust in our relational accounts even if we had no money in the bank. All of our company financial accounts had already been transferred to the soon-to-be-defunct Chipshot.com with zero chance of clawing back any of the money. So, we told our team we planned to start the company over, raise money, and make things whole. But there were no guarantees, of course, and oh, by the way, no money to cover their payroll until we funded our mulligan.

We figured most of them would be shocked and angry and walk out, probably to the nearest bar. Not one person left. That was a pretty awesome and overwhelming feeling, and it taught us a major lesson about the importance of transparency with employees which we would bring to all our future companies.

We then hit the road again, startup style, on our dime. We needed money fast.

First stop: San Francisco. We shared a room in a motel that had bulletproof glass in the reception window. The only redeeming trait was that it had two queen beds. Our freshly signed marital vows did not involve sharing a bed with Caspar.

Next stop: New York City, where we stayed with Kass's Aunt Maureen, or "Aunt Boo" as everyone affectionately called her (RIP dear Aunt Boo), in her 900-square-foot one-bedroom apartment on the Upper East Side—Caspar on the couch, us on the Murphy bed, and Aunt Boo in her bedroom.

We did whatever we could to raise money without spending money, and frankly, we created some of our fondest memories along the way.

We hustled hard and worked (and networked) smart. But we also caught a few breaks without which we would have ended up looking for traditional jobs. Like when we met a golf-obsessed venture capitalist, Keith Bank, who had just started his firm, KB Partners, and was based in the suburbs of Chicago!

Keith, who has now played the top 100 courses in the world, not only backed us but also introduced us to Bill Weaver, a lawyer and ardent golfer who happened to sit on the board of the legendary Medinah Country Club.

Bill was one of the few people in Chicago at the time who truly believed in the power of the Internet to transform business and society. As his tech entrepreneur client and friend, Andrew "Flip" Filipowski told the *Chicago Tribune* after Bill's passing, "He was the first guy to, in a special way, comprehend the opportunity that technology and software represented in this geography and was the preeminent guy working with a lot of entrepreneurs who were trying to build businesses back then."*

Meeting Bill was one of the luckiest moments of our career. He organized a meeting for us with his wealthy golfing friends where we raised about $1 million while eating lunch at Medinah, a club that has hosted multiple major championships. (Bill received no commission, and his only requirement was that we use his firm, Sachnoff & Weaver, for legal work. No problem, Bill!)

We left that lunch meeting feeling like we had just sunk a thirty-foot putt from the fringe of the green for a birdie! We were making progress with our fundraising goal.

Our original angel investors—again, mostly family members and friends—had the option to reinvest, and this time at an even lower valuation. Several re-invested, but many felt burned and didn't want to throw what they saw as good money away after a bad deal. We understood.

It took about three months, but we raised $3 million in fresh capital. We were proud, but the deal was bittersweet due to the significant collateral damage from the failed Chipshot.com deal. We lost relationships forever, including investors who never returned our calls. And we owned much less of the company than in the original iteration because we had to sell more than 50 percent of the equity to fund GolfServ 2.0.

---

* Goldsborough, Bob. "William N. Weaver Jr., 1934-2013." *Chicago Tribune*, December 23, 2018. https://www.chicagotribune.com/2014/01/05/william-n-weaver-jr-1934-2013-2/.

Nonetheless, like many times in our career, we did what we had to do to get to the next level. We used some of the money to purchase the Golf.com domain from NBC Sports and spent the next five (exhausting) years building the largest golf-focused internet media company at the time while simultaneously building our new marriage and a young family that soon included the first two of our three kids.

In June 2005, we were staying with Aunt Boo again in New York for sales meetings (and to escape the kids for a few days!). We met one of our investors at his private tennis club on the East Side. We had no idea such things even existed. The River Club counted many great business leaders as members—names you may recognize, such as Astor, Rockefeller, Vanderbilt, and Morgan. While Kass was beating our investor in ping pong, Mike received an email from our contact at Time Warner. She asked for our fax number to send us an offer to buy the business.

Mike sent her the club's fax number. Minutes later, we made our way to the club's dusty management office. Several pieces of wax fax paper, still warm from the transmission and beginning to curl, outlined the details of Time Warner's offer to buy Golf.com for $24 million. (The irony of receiving a fax to buy an early internet company while inside a club frequented by entrepreneurs who built the country's transportation, communications, and finance industries was not lost on us.)

We had done it. Even though our windfall wasn't enormous based on the standards of today's tech deals, it was the turning point in our professional journey. When we closed the sale in January 2006, our combined founders' share of approximately $3 million turned into the seed we needed to grow additional companies and the money to buy a bigger apartment for our expanding family.

The investors who supported us after the Chipshot.com debacle were thrilled, and, most importantly for us, the employees who stuck with us received well-deserved proceeds from the sale. No one left filthy rich, but no one left covered in crap either. We were now off and running with a bag full of lessons.

Not long after selling Golf.com, twenty months later to be exact, we launched Buddy Media, our biggest and best-known startup success story. We grew it into the world's leading social media marketing platform and sold it to Salesforce in 2012 for $745 million. But our journey to Buddy Media and beyond didn't just begin with Golf.com. It began years earlier in the entrepreneurial origins that shaped our lives and brought us together.

ENTREPRENEURIAL ORIGINS

THE CRAP WE'RE BORN INTO IS THE CRAP FROM WHICH WE GROW.

At least seven varieties of mushrooms grow in poop. Some are poisonous. None are typically served as food. One species, *Psilocybe cubensis*, or "magic mushrooms," often germinates in cow, horse, or buffalo dung. Eat enough of these and you'll likely experience an alternative reality complete with nausea and vomiting.

In other words, it's a lot like the life of an entrepreneur.

The point is, a lot of interesting things grow out of crap—flowers, vegetables, and entrepreneurs. The crap entrepreneurs are born into (along with sunshine and water) helps form what they eventually become. These life experiences help drive them to launch and build a company and give them the assorted skills and mindset needed to survive and succeed.

To fully appreciate and get the most from the lessons we've learned as entrepreneurs, we think it helps to know a little about the soil from which our lives and careers sprouted.

Our backgrounds are similar and different. We are the first to acknowledge that we were both born in well-established gardens. We often say that we are among the luckiest people in the world. We come from upper-middle-class families where education was a priority and money was ample enough to cover our private school tuition and annual vacations.

The soil, however, wasn't perfect. There were weeds, and we didn't always get the right mix of sun and water. But our unique backgrounds, advantages, and challenges shaped us as entrepreneurs and nurtured a similar drive to work hard. Along the way, we merged into a family and formed a partnership that has served us well in business and life.

SURVIVING IN DYSFUNCTION—KASS

I grew up in the Northern Virginia suburbs near Washington, DC. My father, Ralph Savarese, was a well-known antitrust trial attorney with a high-power law firm (Howrey & Simon). My mother, also extremely intelligent, was one of a handful of women offered a scholarship to study under the famed economist Milton Friedman. Instead, she married my father and moved to Ann Arbor, Michigan, where my dad was doing a law fellowship.

My mother was an incredible cook, and I spent much of my childhood learning from her in the kitchen. I was amazed by her instincts and confidence. She never disappointed, even in the simplest of meals. I learned all of my cooking skills from her.

I also inherited my love of holidays from her, especially Halloween and Christmas.

When it came to decorating for Christmas, Mom had no rivals. She had a tree in every common room with different themes and ornaments (often made by her) that matched the room's color. As a result, Christmastime was and still is my favorite holiday. I call it "my Super Bowl," and I believe that's because of my mom.

She also went all out for Halloween. Our costumes were handmade and our house was always one of the best-decorated in our neighborhood. Let's just say we had long lines of trick-or-treaters every year.

When my mom had a gathering, the decor tied into a theme, whether a holiday or some special occasion. I loved those occasions and took a similar approach to our celebrations with employees throughout the years.

My dad got to be my "fun parent." When I was ten, he became the managing partner of his firm, which meant spending less time in the courtroom and much more quality time with me than he had been able to with my three older siblings.

I waited with anticipation for him to come home from work so we could throw the ball in the backyard. On special nights he let me stay up a bit later to look at the stars, and I would zip into his sweater to keep warm. As a former college basketball and tennis player, he definitely gave me my love of sports (basketball, tennis, and golf, to name a few).

Dad also coached me in athletics and helped amplify my competitiveness (although I am pretty sure I walked out of my mom's womb competitive). He taught me the discipline it took to succeed in athletics, and eventually, I translated that into business. He modeled the virtues of being prepared, consistent practice, and hard work, often using words like *tenacity* and *grit* that I adopted as part of my mantra in life.

While I benefited greatly from the influence of my parents, my childhood was far from idyllic, and the good and the dysfunctional combined to shape me into the entrepreneur, friend, wife, and mother I would become.

My mom battled severe anxiety for much of her life, coupled with what I look back on now as depression and loneliness. She raised four children without any babysitters while my dad was either working late hours or on the road nonstop with trials. She was beyond exhausted, and the grind that got to her inevitably spilled onto the rest of the family.

Having my own kids now, I don't know how she did it. But as a child, navigating my mom's mental health was a rocky and uncertain task. I never knew which mom I would wake up to; her moods were volatile, and her fuse could be short.

As the youngest with a five-and-a-half-year age gap to my closest sibling, I was often on my own while my siblings did what older kids do—not play with their baby sister. My mom's favorite line to me was, "Go outside and play." And if I wasn't outside, I was in my room, by choice or by force.

I was sent to my room often as a child, usually because Mom said I was sassy (I was) or annoying (I was bored). Once, when I was around eight or nine years old, Mom sent me to my room because I had asked for something too many times (I was, in fact, a "nudge," as my family called me). She marched me to my room, pulled me over to my bed, and left saying, "Don't come out until you figure out what's wrong with you and why you don't listen."

It was confusing at the time, and I decided to try and never say anything like that to my own kids, but I didn't think something was wrong with me. I just knew something wasn't necessarily right with my mom. Looking back, I don't think she was entirely fulfilled as a mom, although she never confirmed that with me. She came from a generation that expected her to marry, be a "good wife," and raise children. There was no thought of her wants or needs or of the opportunities that opened up for her after college that she had to decline.

My parents were unhappily married for forty-two years. My siblings and I found ourselves stuck in the middle of their parental wars, having to choose sides with no real "winner." We were definitely not a team, and the severe lack of family cohesiveness only escalated after my siblings left for college.

Mom and Dad divorced a few months after Mike and I married in 1999. My only question at the time was: what took them so long? But something good grew out of the intensity, sadness, and uncertainty of my childhood.

I became self-sufficient, for instance, and never feared that I couldn't figure things out on my own. Whether it was the business hustles I started during college (I decorated homes for the holidays to earn money and made a real repeat business out of it), or competition in sports, I always bet on myself. I was a self-starter who prided myself on working hard and achieving what I set out to accomplish.

I also learned to sit in the shit and be with it. By surviving it, I developed a strong sense of self-confidence and a determination to pursue my personal career goals, have a loving marriage, and build a cohesive family (at home and at work).

I applied those virtues to my academics, but that part of my life didn't come easily, and I learned later in life (at age thirty-eight!) that I was dyslexic. When I was in school, all I knew was that it seemed like I had to work harder than many other students to get the grades I wanted. I wasn't upset by this; I liked hard work. And

I somehow got into Dartmouth College thanks to being recruited to play on the tennis team.

I made some lifelong friends at Dartmouth, but I did not love the overall college experience as much as I wish I had.

While Dartmouth is a prestigious and historic university, the campus is in rural Hanover, New Hampshire. I was glad to be on my own, but there was some culture shock for someone from a large suburb of a major city. I also found the course load difficult to manage with my athletic commitments (and what I now realize was my dyslexia). Plus, like many universities across the country at the time, the school still had a bit of the frat boy "bro culture" popularized in the 1978 movie *Animal House*. This was very different from how my father raised my sister and me—as equals to all men, including our brothers.

Nonetheless, my time at Dartmouth proved formative in many important ways, including fine-tuning my time-management and multitasking skills and teaching me lessons I would later use when navigating the mostly male golf industry at GolfServ.

By the time I graduated from college, I knew I wanted a career, and I knew the types of people I wanted to work with, but I was a bit lost as to what to do next.

I should have known I would eventually run my own companies. I had seen my dad lead a major law firm and the allure of shaping an organization appealed to me. I loved the operations side of businesses, loved taking on several things at one time, valued excellence, and had a highly tuned sense of independence because of my childhood. But I didn't immediately jump into the entrepreneurial waters.

Instead, my professional life began with a short stint as a consultant with IMC (thanks to a connection from my dad), and I quickly realized management consulting wasn't a fit for me.

I had been with IMC for a few years when I got a call from Jay Jaffe, a DC-based entrepreneur whose company, Jaffe & Associates, provided marketing services to the nation's largest law firms. I had met him several times through my dad, whose firm was a client. I told Jay I had just created IMC's first website using HotDog Pro software. Then, I casually suggested he use the internet to help market law firms, a novel idea at the time. Intrigued, he called the next day and offered me a role leading a new division building websites for his law firm clients.

I had been making $26,500 a year at IMC. Jay doubled my salary. More importantly, he gave me my first real taste of the entrepreneur's life. I was in charge of starting this new division from scratch. And I liked the challenge of going from zero to one. I worked hard and enjoyed figuring out the processes and operations necessary to build and sell "cutting-edge" web services to law firms. I enjoyed the financial rewards and the positive feedback I had become addicted to during my years on the tennis and basketball courts.

I enjoyed my time at Jaffe, but I left in November 1997 to move to Chicago to be with Mike. I went to work for GiantStep, a firm owned by the ad agency Leo Burnett that provided website development services to large companies like United Airlines. While I liked the work, I wanted more when it came to culture. I also wanted ownership, an actual slice of the pie. And this fueled my fire to create a company and run it my way.

These early work experiences influenced my path in business. But most of my motivation came from my childhood. I had a strong desire to fulfill something that I believe sprung from the lack of control and cohesiveness I had felt in my family system.

I learned to be OK with myself (who I was and what I had in life) while searching for control and satisfaction in other areas of life—my very small friend groups and hobbies, for instance. And as a leader of a business—and my own businesses, in particular—I saw that I could influence not only the success of the company, but the culture. It was a chance to build environments at work that were stable, responsive, and everything else I felt had been missing while growing up and from my previous work experiences.

I knew I was capable of starting my own business. Still, it would be a few more years before I put all my chips on the table as an entrepreneur.

For that to happen, I needed someone else to bet on—and someone who would bet on me. I needed Mike.

FUNCTIONALLY DYSFUNCTIONAL—MIKE

Compared to Kass, I grew up on Easy Street. My parents divorced when I was six, sparing me and my two brothers the domestic turmoil that dominated Kass's childhood. While Kass describes her family as dysfunctional, I describe mine as functionally dysfunctional. My childhood was far from idyllic, but it worked. I felt loved and supported.

I grew up around entrepreneurs, but not the type Kass and I would become.

David Lazerow, my paternal grandfather, was an optometrist who ran his practice from his suburban Baltimore basement. Grandpa Dave worked hard at his practice but also often traveled the world with my entrepreneurial grandmother, Hessie, a travel agent. Their decisions to work for themselves provided a level of independence I admired.

My mother's father, Harry Myerberg, or Pop Pop, was also an entrepreneur, and my role model. After spending a few years in New York City working with four brothers he knew from Baltimore—Harry, Albert, Sam, and Jack Warner, better known now as the Warner Bros.—Pop Pop took his father's advice and went to work in the family's nascent real estate business.

Pop Pop found his true calling as a developer. Over the next seventy years he built more than twelve thousand apartments, townhomes, single-family homes, and several strip malls. Nonetheless, I am most proud of his philanthropy and civil rights activism. Pop Pop met with former First Lady Eleanor Roosevelt after World War II to discuss ways to integrate construction work sites racially. He was one of the first builders to do so.

Pop Pop and I were very close, and I sat with him in February 2006 as he passed at the ripe young age of ninety-eight. He was my biggest fan, believing in me before I believed in myself. He was one of two people who encouraged me to launch U-Wire as a sophomore at Northwestern (the other being my advisor, Mary Dedinsky). Pop Pop's $5,000 investment into the venture funded the purchase of an Apple Macintosh PowerBook Series 500 laptop. It was a brick of a machine that weighed more than today's desktops, but it gave me the independence to work on U-Wire from anywhere on Northwestern's campus.

Turning land into buildings is clearly in my blood because my father, Arthur Lazerow, also started out in the construction business. We spent Saturdays together, often visiting his development projects in Frederick, Maryland. And I remember being proud of him when he won a local Builder of the Year award.

My dad taught me the hard way how important it is for entrepreneurs to focus on and maintain their mental health. Shortly before my thirteenth birthday, Dad's business was underwater. He had underestimated the cost of developing one of his projects and faced a severe cash crunch. The stress from the situation caused a complete mental breakdown weeks before my Bar Mitzvah. My stepmother, a compassionate physical therapist working in the DC area, saved his life by checking him into a psychiatric hospital where he was able to get the help he needed.

I have spent much of my life angry with my dad about how he handled his business issues. But as I have processed the experience, I feel an overwhelming gratitude. I learned important lessons at an early age from my dad's business and mental health challenges that have shaped who I am today. I saw the dangers of debt and the toll companies can take on entrepreneurs' lives. And I learned to deal with issues as they come so they don't stack up like books, eventually tumbling down on you.

After his recovery, my dad launched one of the largest home inspection companies in the DC area and dabbled in other entrepreneurial ventures. He was also a long-time volunteer and leader at Maryland's crisis hotline. He helped thousands who were struggling with their mental health to get the support and treatment they needed.

Meanwhile, my mom remarried a family friend, Harold Zirkin, who was also an entrepreneur. After graduating from Syracuse University, Harold started a money management firm and helped raise me and my brothers like his own sons. We remain very close, and much of our relationship has always involved discussing sports and businesses of all types.

Despite those entrepreneurial influences, my original path had nothing to do with business. I went to Northwestern University to become a journalist. The school was far from my first choice. I applied to five schools, and only Northwestern admitted me. I am a big believer in things happening for a reason, even if you don't know the reason at the time. As it turned out, Northwestern was the perfect school for me, and my life changed for the better.

I wrote for *The Daily Northwestern* as a freshman and did internships in DC for *Roll Call*, which has been covering the political scene on Capitol Hill since 1955.

As a senior about to graduate from college, *Roll Call* offered me a full-time job. My mother, at the time a civil rights lobbyist for the American Association of University Women, thought I was "born" to be a journalist and wanted me to return to our hometown to cover politics. She had no doubt I was the next Bob Woodward (or at least Carl Bernstein). However, my experience with the internet gave me doubts about the newspaper industry's future, which showed no signs of adapting to the new way people would create and receive information using technology. Plus, I was hooked on the idea of building companies.

Should I take a job making $20,000 a year for a newspaper? Or stick with U-Wire, where I was the boss, making good money for a college student but not enough to fund a life?

In this case, my heart played a big factor in the decision, but not in the way you might suspect. I was born with a congenital heart defect, a hole between the two ventricles of my heart, and at eighteen months old, I went into heart failure. Today, it would be a relatively simple fix (most likely without opening one's chest). Back then, not so much. You just prayed.

The good news is that someone's prayers were answered and the hole closed miraculously before my second birthday. Other than the regular trips to the cardiologist, I had a relatively normal childhood. Went to school. Played on a few sports teams and in the high school band. Wrote for the student newspaper. Made decent grades. Eventually, I went to college and started U-Wire—standard stuff, except for maybe the business part.

In 1994, between my sophomore and junior years in college, my cardiologist discovered that the hole in my heart hadn't fully closed when I was a baby and was starting to open up again. He recommended open-heart surgery to fix it. Since I was young and otherwise healthy, he told me I should have the surgery that summer. I called Mort Kondracke, the editor of *Roll Call* who had offered me an internship, and told him I had other plans for the summer.

During the procedure the surgeon also found and repaired damage to my aortic valve. That was good news. The bad news came eight days later during a post-surgery checkup. My doctor discovered, to his horror, that I had zero blood pressure. He went into emergency mode and called the nearby Georgetown University Hospital to tell them I was on my way for an urgent valve replacement.

"No time for an ambulance," he screamed to my mom. "Get him to the hospital right now because he's about to die!"

My repaired aortic valve had burst, and I had a three-hour window to replace the valve to keep me alive.

On the way to the hospital I asked my mom if we could stop to get sushi before having my chest cracked open for the second time in two weeks. Yes, I had close to zero blood pressure. But other than slight dizziness, blurred vision, and a general sense of listlessness that hadn't waned since the surgery, I felt great! My mom wasn't buying it and reassured me with something loving like, "Shut up, you f'ing asshole." I thought that response was a bit much as I had been told before the checkup that I could finally eat whatever I wanted.

Minutes later, Dr. Richard Hopkins took out my faulty valve and put in a St. Jude No. 25 Artificial Valve as my mom downed a bottle of white wine by herself in the hospital waiting room.

I awoke from the surgery to find Rabbi Joe Weinberg, the esteemed senior rabbi of the Washington Hebrew Congregation, standing next to me in full black-tie garb. I assumed I was dead, and Rabbi Joe was there to meet me as I passed to whatever comes next. But he was there to recite the *Mi Shebeirach*, a Jewish prayer for healing, before he headed to a Bar Mitzvah that evening.

Spoiler alert! Despite my heart's best attempt to do me in, I made it. Even at nineteen, I knew I was now playing in extra innings. It was a key moment of clarity for me. Most of the worries and social anxieties that I'd been carrying went away after I woke up from the surgery. I felt a new sense of fearlessness. I wasn't reckless, but I didn't want to waste whatever time came my way. Seeing my death gave me an appreciation for life—one that I have to this day, and that empowers me during even the darkest and most challenging times.

It also gave me the courage to pivot toward entrepreneurship. I wasn't sure I wanted to run U-Wire for the rest of my life, but I was captivated by the internet. It was the great unknown. That's where I wanted to go. I was only missing one thing: the right person to join me on the adventure. Thankfully, that soon changed.

A MATCH MADE IN EMAIL HEAVEN

Our earliest interactions were infrequent and uneventful. While I (Kass) grew up in Virginia, Mike lived across the river in Bethesda,

Maryland. I am a little more than three years older, or, as Mike, says, "She's a cougar." But I went to school in the 1980s with Mike's sister Leslie and I was close friends with his older brother, Andrew.

In November 1996, nine years after we first met (in the basement of Mike's home while I was hanging out with his brother and our friends), we spent considerable time together in Allentown, Pennsylvania, at the wedding of our mutual dear friends Kevin and Jill Kane.

Our attraction was more than physical, though a close friend at the wedding says the electricity between us was palpable. We had *it,* whatever *it* was. While we had spent very little time together over the years, we gave a joint toast at the rehearsal dinner, and several guests approached us afterward to ask how long we had been together.

I (Mike) thought (and still think) that Kass is beautiful and sexy. But her inner strength and interest in innovation and the early internet intrigued me. I also appreciated her lack of pretense during what I now consider our first date: shoe shopping in the Redding, Pennsylvania, outlet stores (Kass had forgotten to bring formal shoes for the wedding), followed by hotdogs and shakes at Dairy Queen! I had always been attracted to smart, tough, attractive, and driven women who apparently also love junk food.

I have no plans to recap my unsuccessful dives into the dating pool (though such a recap would indeed be short due to my intense fear of asking out girls, an unfortunate byproduct of my single-sex education). But trust me when I say I was beyond thrilled that Kass took the lead in emailing after Jill and Kevin's wedding (one of many times that Kass took the lead on something, and it worked out!).

hi mike,

this is a test. i know you thought i wouldn't write. but i guess i couldn't resist. hope you had a safe trip back.
    2 things: 1) your business card says founder . . . hmmmm . . . interesting. what does this mean? and 2) I wore the shoes the other night to a business function. I love them. You have a good eye . . . or is it eyes!?

-kass

It was clear even to twenty-two-year-old me and the feeble emotional intelligence housed in my immature brain that Kass wasn't just another girl for me to date. She was a woman of strength. I had never met anyone like her, and I was hooked. So, after a week of emailing I decided to surprise her (or maybe Kass convinced me, I can't remember!) by booking a flight back to DC where she was living.

After our weekend together, in which I tried (unsuccessfully) to hide my visit from my many family members in the area, I landed back in Chicago with another email from Kass. She thanked me for "the most incredible, wonderful weekend" and then made it clear that "this in no way confirms at all that I have a crush on you, just in case you were wondering. :)"

Gotta love a woman who keeps all her options open!

Less than three years after we first danced together at Kevin and Jill's wedding, I sent Kass another email that would change our lives forever.

It was March 13, 1999, and by now Kass had moved to Chicago, quit her job at GiantStep, and started GolfServ with me and

Mike Caspar. We got up and headed to Saturday brunch at our favorite Mexican joint, Uncle Julio's, the same place we would take the GolfServ employee "survivors" for margaritas and fajitas after each of our many layoffs. It was our happy place and the happy place of many of our employees. We then headed back to the office.

The NCAA basketball tournament was in full swing, so I excused myself and went to our apartment above our office to watch a game. Before I left, however, I hit "send" on an email I thought would get a quick and positive reaction.

> *kass-*
>
> *I figured our relationship started on email, so why not take the next step on email. I love you and want you to be my roommate, best friend, business partner, mother of my dog, lover and WIFE for the rest of my life.*
> *Love you, and please say yes!*
>
> *-me*

Five minutes passed. Nothing.
Ten minutes. Nothing.
Twenty minutes. Nothing.

The long wait should not have been a surprise. I had long appreciated Kass's methodical and structured approach to email (and pretty much everything she does)—a process that ensures nothing falls through the cracks. Ever. So, while I awaited a response to the most important question I have ever asked, Kass slowly worked through her inbox in the order the emails had arrived, responding as necessary to the twenty or thirty missives from accountants and lawyers.

Eventually, she got to my message. Swept off her feet (my take on it), she rushed upstairs to our apartment where Cookie (our Bernese Mountain Dog rescue) and I were watching basketball.

Kass: "Are you f'ing kidding me? An email?"

Shocked but not surprised at my non-traditional approach to marriage proposals, she thought my email was super clever, or at least that's how I took it. And you already know how she responded; this book wouldn't exist if she hadn't said yes.

In defense against those who refuse to acknowledge the dorky romance in my approach, rest assured that my plan for the rest of the day was more analog than digital. "Pack a bag," I told Kass. I had a suite waiting for us at the Four Seasons (with a bathtub because our apartment didn't have one) on Michigan Avenue and dinner at Spiaggia, the nicest Italian restaurant in Chicago (that we could afford).

We tied the knot later that year in Florida at Kass's parents' vacation home and continued the theme of mixing our work lives with our personal lives. Rather than going to the Caribbean for our honeymoon, we flew across the country to La Jolla, California. First, we didn't want to be in the Caribbean during the end of hurricane season. And second, we knew we could get more work done in California.

This was October 1999, and we were negotiating the terms of our ill-fated deal with Chipshot.com, so we had to do what we had to do. As we quickly learned, this is all part of the imbalanced life that comes with being entrepreneurs.

THE IMBALANCED LIFE

THE CRAP THAT COMES WITH THE PRESSURES ON YOUR PERSONAL LIFE.

It was April 4, 2004, and I (Kass) rested uncomfortably on a gurney at Sibley Memorial Hospital in Washington, DC, following the birth of our second child.

The long day had begun the night before. Mike convinced me to stop unpacking and hanging pictures at our new home in Rockville, Maryland long enough to go to a movie. So, I brushed off the weird signals my body gave out and snacked on popcorn and Sno-Caps (my favorites) as we watched *Eternal Sunshine of the Spotless Mind*.

Later that night, unable to sleep and feeling nauseous, I wondered if I might be in labor. But I figured I just had a bigger-than-normal bout of indigestion. There had been no noticeable labor with our first son, Myles, back in 2001. Back then, we went to the hospital because my doctor suspected my water had broken a day earlier, and after thirty-eight hours of what my doctor called "unproductive" labor, I had a C-section.

This time, it was still about a week before the doctor had planned to induce labor for what I hoped would be an expected VBAC delivery. But, tired of watching television and unsure why the sickness was getting worse, not better, I called my doctor at 2:30 a.m.—a doctor I'd only met in person once because of our move a few weeks earlier.

"Get to the hospital ASAP," he said.

Mike's father and stepmother came over to stay with Myles, who, thankfully, was snoozing away. We were at Sibley by 3:15 a.m. and in a room about an hour later. I wasn't in severe pain. I was nauseated, but I had work to do around the house and, of course, work to do for our business, which had gone from GolfServ Online to Golf.com after we purchased the domain name from NBC Sports. I soon began making a case to go home.

Nurse: "You're definitely in labor. Look at these contractions here on the monitor. And how about this? It looks like this baby will be born on 04/04/04. How cool is that?"

Numerologists rejoice! I liked the sound of this, so I decided to stay. Little did I know.

When an on-call doctor came by and suggested an epidural to numb the pain from the contractions, I agreed, but it caused far more problems than it solved. Around six a.m., just after getting the injection, I lost all sense of feeling in my entire left side—the left side of my face drooped, and I couldn't raise my left arm. My legs, meanwhile, were becoming numb from the epidural. Later, we learned that the epidural went to my brain and clotted, giving me symptoms of a stroke before it dissolved. When I said something nonsensical to Mike, he began to panic and screamed for help.

I remember thinking, *This is weird. Why doesn't he understand me?*

A gaggle of hospital personnel rushed in and whisked me to an operating room. All I remember was repeatedly mumbling, "APGAR scores, APGAR scores," but no one could understand my slurred request for the test results given to all babies at birth.

Cole soon arrived (seven pounds, five ounces) via an emergency C-section, and his APGAR scores were perfect. He was healthy. I was not.

Mike remained by my side as the doctors now turned their attention to stitching my abdomen back together.

Mike incessantly stroked my head and repeated, "Everything will be OK."

Then, with a suddenly renewed speech capacity, I shouted, "Get the f*$k off me!"

"Yeah, OK," Mike said. "She's baaaack, everyone!"

Once he knew Cole and I were both OK, Mike's mind quickly turned to other things, namely, Golf.com. As they wheeled me to the recovery room, exhausted and wondering if my face would permanently droop like a basset hound's, Mike raised an issue no mother would ever expect to hear just minutes after giving birth.

"I hate to say this right now," Mike said, "but Buick needs their ads up. And I know you know this, but we need to make sure no other auto ads are running at the same time because they have exclusivity."

MASTERING THE MOMENT

Five hundred miles to the south, the world's greatest golfers gathered at Augusta National in preparation for the 68th Masters

Tournament, which was scheduled to begin four days after 04/04/04, Cole's (lucky) day of birth.

Professional golf tournaments, of course, played a huge role in the profitability of Golf.com, and the four major championships were particularly vital to our bottom line. Golf fans came to us for information, and advertisers paid us to access one of the most affluent demographics on the web. So, as Kass gave birth to Cole, the most important ads of our year were scheduled to go live for the week.

While Golf.com had survived four years since we regained ownership, it was still a fledgling enterprise. After 9/11, we scaled back our team to prepare for what we thought would be a deep recession of all things related to travel and luxury. Then, in 2004, with Kass thirty-six weeks pregnant with Cole, we sold the first house we bought together in Chicago to move closer to our extended families in the DC area.

We were running lean—personally and professionally. Unable to afford a home close to the district line, we bought in Rockville, Maryland—thirty minutes from downtown. As R.E.M. pointed out in the song "(Don't Go Back to) Rockville," it was a place "full of filth" and "where nobody says hello."

We actually liked Rockville. But with a new company, a toddler, a large dog, and a baby on the way, the friendliness of our neighbors was the least of our concerns.

Most of what we remember about our twenty-one-month stint in DC is being overworked and limping around like zombies half asleep with no backup resources to help shovel the daily crap. We worked long hours from the 150-square-foot basement office in our new home, and the highlight of our day was driving Myles to a

Montessori school in Chevy Chase, Maryland in our manual-shift Mini Cooper. Buying groceries afforded one of us a few minutes to interact with other adult humans outside our nuclear family.

Our margin for error with Golf.com was nonexistent. If Mike didn't sell ads, we would have no revenue. If Kass didn't traffic those ads and manage the advertisers and agencies, again, no revenue. And if Caspar didn't keep the site up so we could serve the ads, you guessed it, no revenue.

So, when Cole's early arrival coincided with the 2004 Masters week, Mike tried his best to cover for me. He knew what needed to be done with the Buick ads but had no idea how to do it. This was before YouTube and other online videos, which today provide instant instruction on just about everything.

Careful not to interfere with the tubes and probes attached to me, Mike reached over the hospital bed's side guardrails and placed a laptop gently on my recently stitched abdomen.

I logged into DoubleClick, a management platform used by advertisers and agencies, and turned on the ads to ensure we didn't miss those vital revenues. I then returned my attention to our new bundle of joy and my recovery as Mike commented how lucky he was to have such a motivated, tough, and committed partner.

The Masters, meanwhile, went on as scheduled, clearly unaware of all that was going on in our personal and professional lives. Phil Mickelson, however, wasn't the only one who cashed in that week. We couldn't match his $1.17 million paycheck, but it was the most profitable week in our brief history.

The successful week helped us exceed $2 million in annual revenue in 2004 for the first time in Golf.com's history, setting us on a path to sell the company. Thank you, Phil (and Tiger Woods), for capturing the world's attention, and to Cole and Myles for providing us the motivation to get Golf.com over the goal line.

SOWING AND REAPING

This might not be a universal law along the same lines as sowing and reaping, but we know from experience that there is never a good time for entrepreneurs to have children. Not for us and not for you. But don't blame the children. They are reaped from what you've sown, so to speak.

Children were (and are!) important to us. You may not want kids. And that's fine. But if you are running your own business, you need to know that you will pay a price for doing anything important to you, just as sure as we paid a price for chasing our startup dreams while starting a family.

An entrepreneur's personal life inevitably conflicts with the endless stream of work. There is no off switch. No quiet quitting. No balance. There's only an effort to manage the imbalance as effectively as you can.

Here's the hard reality: you can't have it all.

I (Kass) believe you can only do one thing at a time really well. If starting and growing a business is *the one thing*, other things (like your closest relationships) will suffer. And when other priorities are more important, the business will suffer. During these inevitable trade-offs, your friendships, family, and health inevitably get something less than your best.

If you aren't willing to embrace and deal with these realities, that's OK. But if that's the case, we recommend you don't become an entrepreneur. If you are willing, however, don't let the imbalance cost you a dime more than you absolutely have to pay.

In many respects, we were intentional and strategic about the sacrifices that came with our career choices. We talked openly about sacrificing time with our kids during their early childhoods in hopes of getting time back with them when they were older. We were focused on financial success to provide our children (and others we could impact through philanthropy) with a better life.

There's a risk in this because, as too many entrepreneurs can attest, you can easily get consumed by the work and wake up one day with grown kids (and grandkids) you hardly know; the window for reclaiming time with them already closed. That wasn't the case for us, but hindsight confirms that we could have done better. While we couldn't avoid an imbalanced life, we could have suffered less and enjoyed the journey a little more.

JUGGLING FAMILY PRIORITIES

It would be great to say the story of Cole's birth was an anomaly in our lives as entrepreneurs, but in reality, it reflects the norm. Thirty-plus years after starting our first companies, we realize that coordinating life and company events is impossible.

We've already shared how our work intertwined with our engagement and honeymoon, and the timing of our children's births coincided with some significant business events.

Our first child, Myles, arrived on December 21, 2001, just a few months after the 9/11 attacks sent the country (and Golf.com) into full-on chaotic survival mode. We were so busy that Kass took less than a week of maternity leave.

After Myles and Cole, there was Viv. Our daughter showed up on May 24, 2007, which happened to be the same day Facebook held its first F8 conference at the San Francisco Design Center.

Mark Zuckerberg unveiled the Facebook Platform, and the company called on "all developers to build the next generation of applications with deep integration into Facebook."

Why did that matter to us? Well, after selling Golf.com and moving to New York, I (Mike) stayed with Time Warner for a year as part of the sale terms. But my obligation ended when Viv joined our zoo, and I was scanning the horizon for the next big idea.

After Viv made her entrance at New York's Mount Sinai Hospital, I sat in the recovery room waiting for Kass and read about F8 on my Blackberry device (iPhones debuted a month later!). And with no doctors, nurses, or anesthesia involved, the idea of Buddy Media was born. Then, in a conversation reminiscent of the Buick ads and the 2004 Masters, I shared that idea with Kass as the orderlies rolled her to the recovery room after her third C-section.

I didn't have details of what we would specifically do. I just knew social media and Facebook would be the focus of our next business. Facebook was opening a new phase of the internet. Web 1.0 was a single-player experience. You consumed information on your own island. Web 2.0 was all about friends and connections. *And everything is better*, I thought, *when you are connected to friends*. I wasn't going to let the timing of our third child derail my plans!

Less than three months later, I (Kass) sat on an office floor at the corner of 60th and Columbus Circle in New York City, building Ikea desks for our new company and taking occasional breaks to nurse our daughter.

The arrival of children adds complexities to any family, especially when the parents are entrepreneurs. While we grew our companies, we were also responsible for things like making sure our kids were fed, clothed, and didn't crawl into a busy street. We didn't always give them our best, but we did all we knew in order to give them everything they needed.

Our days took on a draining routine. We got the kids up, fed, and ready in the early mornings. We worked all day. We ate dinner together or attempted to get back in time for their dinner as often as possible. We got the kids to sleep, and we worked some more. As they grew older, things got more complicated and stressful. "Bigger kids, bigger problems," as they say.

We both traveled while running Buddy Media. Mike traveled mainly for sales, fundraising, and speaking, and me for operations. When we acquired a small company in London, I went there with Brittany White, my right-hand operations person and a star employee who was critical in helping us scale and get things up and running.

One of the first emails I read when I arrived at the hotel was from the coach of Cole's soccer team. Mike had failed to ensure that Cole wore the right uniform to one of the season's last games. The coach, an intense parent whose style we weren't fond of, informed us he was kicking Cole off the team for the next season.

In my jetlagged fury, I wrote a rather direct email to the coach who didn't know crap about how to bring out the best in people. My internal mama bear came out, and I might have included something about the coach being an a$$hole and how dare he treat any eight-year-old child, not to mention mine, like this. Instead of sending it to the coach, I sent it to one of our new employees with the same first name. Another great lesson: don't send angry emails without reading them a few times. And never send them jetlagged!

It was a bummer of a mistake, of course, but at least the poop was on my face, not Cole's.

When it came to our imbalanced family/work lives, the worst instances always occurred when life wasn't going well for our children, and we felt like our business duties were either part of the cause or standing in the way of solutions.

When we sold Buddy Media in 2012, Viv was five, Cole was eight, and Myles was ten, so the boys felt the brunt of our absence. Our guess is that they remember that we never missed a play, a rehearsal, or a game, but we often weren't there in the in-between times, and we weren't always fully present or much fun when we were there—we were always tired.

The weekends were good for me because Mike took the kids to get pancakes most Saturdays (which let me get some sleep and quiet, both of which were in short supply). Mike also enjoyed those Saturdays as he loves pancakes and always had fun exploring the city with the kids. When they were young (six and younger), they often went to a park, a kids' concert, a museum, took a ferry ride around New York City, or walked the Highline. As they got older, activities shifted to whacking golf balls and playing mini golf on Randall's Island across the East River or going to a local batting cage.

These Saturday mornings became sacred, as did our regular date night. We knew that we would never prioritize going out as adults if we left planning to the last minute. So as soon as we were able to afford them, we locked down permanent babysitters for Wednesday and Saturday nights (thank you, Jessica Sanchez and Stephanie Alexander). These date nights gave us something to look forward to and helped nourish our relationship.

By blocking the time we didn't need to think about it every week. We just got away. Scheduling date nights is something we highly recommend because if you aren't intentional, they won't happen. And frankly, these date nights gave us time to at least try and talk about something other than business. We weren't always good at that either. We did everything we could to make time to protect our relationship. Date nights were better and less expensive than therapy. Trust us. We have done a lot of both.

The babysitters who delivered became a part of the family. And their family became our family. Nonetheless, they couldn't take the place of us as parents, and that's what made things difficult.

One of the reasons we sold Buddy Media when we did and sold it to Salesforce over other options was because our family life was suffering far beyond what was acceptable. The exit allowed us to course-correct with tremendous financial security and a new owner we believed in and who would support us in the transition.

NURTURING FRIENDSHIPS

A great thing about being an entrepreneur with an ever-present focus on work is that you build deep, meaningful, lifelong relationships with people connected to your work. The downside is that you develop almost no meaningful friendships outside of work.

Families around us who met one another because their kids were in school together would become so close that they went on vacations together. We befriended very few other parents and barely knew the names of our kids' teachers.

One year, at a start-of-school assembly, for instance, the principal told everyone to take their child to their teacher who would be holding a flag with their name on it. Neither of us knew the teachers' names. We hadn't looked that closely at the school emails. And we couldn't ask the other parents because we didn't know them, either. So we wandered around saying, "Here's Viv," and, "Here's Cole," until their teachers corralled us.

Ridiculously embarrassing, to say the least. But when you put everything into your companies, there isn't room to nurture other things, even friendships outside work.

We became very focused on working with people we liked and trusted, so it seemed natural that most of our closest friends were investors, advisors, and clients.

Karin Klein, one of our favorite venture capitalists, led Softbank Ventures' investment into Buddy Media, sat on our board, and shared many life events with us. She has seen our kids grow up, and we are rooting for her as she raises her son Jason as a single mom. And we celebrated Greycroft Partners' Ian Sigalow's marriage, celebrated Bar Mitzvahs of other investors' kids (Roger Ehrenberg), and count many of our investors as close friends.

The same can be said of many of our employees. This is a tricky issue for leaders, as we will discuss in more detail in Chapter 11. Other than our management team members, we generally avoided close, personal relationships with employees. But we got to know and care for the people who worked with us, let them know us, respected them, and enjoyed spending time with them. Deeper friendships often developed after they left the company or after we sold it. And not a week goes by now that we don't talk to one of the Buddies, as Buddy Media employees were known.

Without Buddy Media, we also would not be best friends with Jeff Ragovin (Buddy Media's second employee, later granted "cofounder" status) and his husband Kurt Giehl, who are our sons' godfathers.

But from the beginning of our entrepreneurial journey, we also missed out on relational opportunities that were common to other people. I (Mike) lived in the Phi Gamma Delta (Fiji) fraternity house on the North Campus at Northwestern, but my social life was pretty limited after I launched U-Wire during my sophomore year. The business never turned into a cash cow, but it was profitable early on because I was a one-man shop with few fixed expenses.

Every night at midnight I would bike to *The Daily Northwestern*'s offices in the Norris Student Center with a floppy disk in my pocket to convince someone there to give me *Northwestern*'s stories. Then, I'd ride back to my room, put the stories on my Mac, and combine them with the articles other newspapers sent me via email to go out together as the news service the following day.

One of my roommates and close friends, Seth Meyers (now of *Late Night with Seth Meyers*), remembers the time well. Despite having the lower bunk of one of the two sets of bunk beds, he preferred to sleep on the shared couch, which happened to be against the wall with the only phone jack. Back then, we could only access the internet by plugging our computer into a landline phone jack for the molasses-fast "dial-up" connection.

"I remember how insane it was that you had to wake me up to move the couch and plug into the phone jack," he recently told me. "I never thought it would work. Just don't believe any Silicon Valley garage was a worse starting point than that room was for you."

The experience of juggling school and a company helped me build my executive functioning skills, which are critical for all entrepreneurs. Meanwhile, sleep and partying with friends took a backseat to classes and business (in that order of importance). The only thing that changed after graduation was that I no longer had to go to class. Business became the top priority.

WORKING ON HEALTH AND WELLNESS

While we recognized early on that there would be a price to pay for our entrepreneurial success, there were a few times when we would gladly have taken a mulligan. Neither of us, for instance, took good enough care of ourselves physically, mentally, or emotionally. And that type of imbalance wasn't just bad for us; it hurt our companies.

Starting in the fall of 1996, I (Mike) was constantly in motion—raising money, recruiting, and entertaining clients as I tried (many times unsuccessfully) to sell the product du jour. I even went to Croatia when I ran U-Wire to help foster student journalism in countries that didn't have a free press. And the travel only grew more hectic with Golf.com and Buddy Media.

This resulted in an unhealthy combination of big, rich meals and no exercise. Add in a few drinks with clients (tequila for me at the time), and I ended the day in my room exhausted, only to start the next day with a client meeting over a big breakfast, followed by another full day of work on the run and more food and late-night drinks.

Before I knew it, I was tipping the scales at forty-five pounds heavier than the slender college Mike (and thirty pounds more than where I am today—thank you, Rico Wesley!). I have pictures from those bad old days, but I'm not eager to share them.

I wasn't thinking about diet or exercise. I was just trying to get through each day because we felt the company would not survive if we weren't constantly charging full speed ahead. Maybe the company would have survived. Maybe not. Who knows? But the feeling was real.

Growing up in a family that valued athletics and being fit, I (Kass) began strength training and doing intense cardio when I was around eleven. I played several sports and competed at a high level in tennis in high school (nationally ranked) and in college (D1). I spent my entire life working out. But the busier we got with work and family, the less time I spent on exercise. Soon, there was never even a thought about working out, only about what clothes might fit each morning.

I have always had generalized anxiety, which I used to cope with by exercising daily, deep breathing (I tend to hold my breath a lot), and taking meds. But I wasn't exercising and held my breath most of the time just to get through each day.

As the children grew up, I increasingly wrestled with the guilt of not being there for them. My "operator" brain never turned off. I was obsessed with not allowing anything to fall through the cracks and constantly thinking about caring for our people and creating a positive work culture. Meanwhile, I beat myself up about missing things like Viv's first crawl.

Furthermore, I have always done my best work from five p.m. to two a.m., so my ideal time for work was when other people were spending time with their families or sleeping. And sleeping was a huge issue—more accurately, not sleeping. I never slept for more than an hour at a time or more than three hours a night. When I finally saw a doctor about it during the Buddy Media days, the tests revealed my cortisol level was five times higher than normal, and my adrenal glands were in failure. I was basically in a constant state of fight or flight.

With all of these issues, not to mention the asthma that developed when I was thirty-eight, I knew it was time for me to exit the grind and take better care of myself and our kids. The opportunity to sell Buddy Media came just in time, and Salesforce CEO Marc Benioff agreed to let me go without a penalty while Mike stayed on for many years. (Thank you, Marc, for being so empathetic.)

I remember feeling huge relief when I walked out the door in January 2013, but it took almost another year for me to feel like myself again. My nervous system was totally out of whack, and it took a long, long time to recover from what I believe were PTSD-like symptoms.

IT'S TOO QUIET IN HERE

Many parents have the shared experience of sitting on a comfy couch and soaking in the peace and quiet of the moment only to get hit with an uneasy realization: *This quiet isn't a good quiet. Something must be going on with the kids.* And, more often than not, this intuitive parent alarm sounds an appropriate warning.

The imbalanced life of an entrepreneur can be somewhat like that. Whenever you feel that your personal and professional lives are striking a wonderful balance, something new hits the fan. As the old saying goes, you are either in the middle of a storm, coming out of a storm, or about to enter a storm.

That might seem a little depressing, but the point is that entrepreneurs need to face these realities in a focused, proactive way.

If you want to succeed with a business idea, you have to recognize that there will be very long hours and an endless to-do list that creates tension in your health, your family relationships, and your friendships. So if things seem too quiet, look around for the crap that's either already there or on its way.

Unfortunately, there is no law of the universe that says it all equals out in the end. And even when you do win big, you still might feel the weight of the losses that came in pursuit of victory.

As entrepreneurs, you have a life full of highs and lows that come with sacrifices that often make the wins feel less good. Looking back, we both wish we had celebrated the wins more and been more proactive about addressing the lows.

CUTTING THROUGH THE CRAP: KEY LESSONS LEARNED

This chapter (and those that follow) is full of things we've learned while shoving shit through the years. If you've been underlining or highlighting passages along the way, you can compare your takeaways to these summaries of what we see as the key lessons.

- You can only be good/great at one thing at a time.
- You can't turn the business off. Ever.
- You will sacrifice friendships, family, and health. Entrepreneurship is not balanced; it is just a series of tradeoffs, and none of the tradeoffs are perfect or even good.
- Do whatever you can to make time to care for yourself—mind, body, and soul. If you're broken, the company will be broken.

SAYING "I DO"

PICKING THE RIGHT PARTNERS IS ESSENTIAL FOR DEALING WITH THE CRAP THAT'S COMING YOUR WAY.

When we first danced at Kevin and Jill's wedding in 1996, neither of us was looking for a business partner. But the more time we spent together, the more comfortable we became with the idea that we could build companies together.

Eventually, we both concluded that we were better together than we would have been as solo founders, and the reasons were obvious. Yes, we both loved business and innovation. But our complementary skill sets and shared ethical framework transformed our romance into an equal business partnership.

However, I (Mike) didn't fully appreciate the value of having the right business partner until several years later, when I launched a business with an incompatible cofounder and ended up with a lost friendship and a company in disarray.

My cofounder, Jonathan Cramer, was and is a brilliant artist and one of the most fascinating people you will ever meet. His mind is as powerful as those of the smartest scientists on the planet. And his enormous sculptures and vivid paintings are collected by some of the most prominent patrons in the country. As *New York* magazine described him in 2008, "Think Jackson Pollock, minus the self-destructive alcoholism."[*]

In his spare time, Jonathan invented a visual language based on a mathematical system that emerged from his art. He cut up the eight basic shapes that populate the world—cube, sphere, cylinder, cone, etc.—to create a patented new numeral system known as Shape Matrix that encodes extremely large numbers in a simple-to-read visual system.

Jonathan once showed a 3D model of his system to physicist and mathematician Freeman Dyson at the Institute for Advanced Study in Princeton. The Institute is best known for its School of Mathematics, where Albert Einstein worked for twenty-two years until he died in 1955. Other notable faculty members include J. Robert Oppenheimer, the "father of the atomic bomb," who served as its director for twenty years until he retired in 1966. According to Jonathan and Shape Matrix lore, Freeman immediately grasped the importance of the technology and asked Jonathan how long he had been at the Institute.

"I'm just an artist," Jonathan recalls responding.

Jonathan knew he needed a business partner and resources to develop and commercialize the technology. He and I met every few months, starting around 2011 to discuss Shape Matrix, and I provided light advice. Then, in 2017, after leaving my position at Salesforce, I agreed to his regular request to do more.

---

[*] "50 Sexiest New Yorkers." *New York Magazine*, accessed April 20, 2024. https://nymag.com/news/articles/03/08/sexiest/50newyorkers/7.htm.

Jonathan and I created Shape Operating System, Inc. to bring the Shape Matrix invention to market and raised $1.5 million to get the business started. Most of the funds came from Kass and my previous investors, and the rest came from a few of Jonathan's finance friends. Then we built an initial prototype of two potential commercial applications. The first, Shapecode, replaced passwords with geometric shapes that were easier for people to remember but hard for hackers to compromise. The second, Shapetag, was an advanced QR code-like visual system that allowed for secure tracking of goods of any size or material.

We also recruited several key team members. The most important were Ted Theisen and Nick Petraco. Ted was a former FBI special agent and chief of cyber integrity for the executive office of the president and White House under President Obama. And Nick was a salt-of-the-earth former police detective with forty years of experience as a criminalist with the NYPD's trace evidence lab. He had authored five textbooks and more than 160 scientific papers on forensic science, crime scene investigation, and forensic microscopy. He would be an integral part of our efforts to apply tagging solutions to physical materials.

Investors continued to be excited, and eventually, we raised $13 million for Shape Matrix. Despite conversations with more than thirty companies about licensing Shapetag and Shapecode, we were unable to generate any revenue—zero dollars. One reason for this was the dysfunctional relationship between the cofounders: Jonathan and me.

START WITH THE RIGHT QUESTION

When it comes to the structure for founding a new company, most advice we see focuses on the wrong questions: *Should I have a cofounder? If so, how many? Is it wise for my spouse or significant other to be a cofounder? Why not be a solo founder?*

The data shows you can succeed or fail no matter your route. Eighty percent of all billion-dollar startups have had at least two founders, according to research by Ali Tamaseb, author of *Super Founders*.[*] Research by Jason Greenberg (NYU) and Ethan Mollick (Wharton), meanwhile, shows that companies with solo founders survive longer, generate more revenue, and perform about the same financially as companies with founding teams.[†]

Statistics about which route has proven more successful are mostly irrelevant in our opinions. What matters is picking the *right* partner(s) if you have cofounders and gathering the *right* people around you if you are a solo founder. And because we happen to be married and successful as business partners, we can confidently tell you that finding the right cofounder is very much like finding the right spouse or life partner.

When you start a business with someone, you essentially marry that person. Your cofounder becomes the first person you talk to once your workday begins, the last person you talk to about the business each night, your roommate when you travel, someone to commiserate with when things go poorly, and the one you celebrate with when things go great. You're peas and carrots. Inseparable.

---

[*] Tamaseb, Ali. "Land of the Super Founders: A Data-Driven Approach to Uncover the Secrets of Billion Dollar Startups." *Medium*, December 5, 2018. https://alitamaseb.medium.com/land-of-the-super-founders-a-data-driven-approach-to-uncover-the-secrets-of-billion-dollar-a69ebe3f0f45.

[†] Greenberg, Jason, and Ethan Mollick. "Sole Survivors: Solo Ventures Versus Founding Teams." *ResearchGate*, January 2018. https://www.researchgate.net/publication/323198610_Sole_Survivors_Solo_Ventures_Versus_Founding_Teams.

Instead of signing a one-page marriage certificate, cofounders sign a thick stack of legal papers—partnership and incorporation documents, bylaws, confidentiality agreements, and invention assignments. Cofounders are legally bound, for better or worse, in corporate sickness and health. And this is before the business generates its first dollar in revenue.

If you see that as a vast, unwelcome ball at the end of your chain, you may want to start your business yourself. That's a perfectly fine option. No law requires an entrepreneur to have a cofounder, and solo founders launched several great companies—Amazon (Jeff Bezos), Dell (Michael Dell), Alibaba (Jack Ma), and Oracle (Larry Ellison), among many others.

Solo founders have the freedom—and responsibility!—to make decisions independently without the friction of debate. They set their vision, execute on their terms, and retain 100 percent of the equity at the onset.

Life as a solo founder, however, will not be without challenges. Expect to be lonely. Expect to bear much pressure that your friends and family might not understand. Your decision-making will often be limited to only one perspective (yours!), which can lead to paralysis or bad calls. And your company will be more vulnerable—if something happens to you, the company may not survive.

I (Mike) have often considered whether my dad would have felt better and made different decisions if he had a cofounder to help him shovel. There is no way to know for sure but I believe things would have turned out differently.

TAKING THE TEAM BUS

Plenty of successful companies were cofounded by partners who, like us, were (or are) romantically involved. The babies of such unions include Cisco Systems (Len Bosack and Sandy Lerner), Marvell Technology (Sehat Sutardja and Weili Dai), Houzz (Adi Tatarko and Alon Cohen), Clif Bar & Company (Kit Crawford and Gary Erickson), and JB Hunt Transport Services (Johnnie Bryan and Johnelle Hunt). Those companies alone have a combined market capitalization of more than $280 billion!

Partnerships bring diverse skill sets to the leadership table, shared responsibility, emotional support, collaborative decision-making, a broader network, and more resources. You can also expect a higher level of commitment from cofounders than employees because founders have more skin in the game.

This model has worked out well for us, not to mention companies like Google (Larry Page and Sergey Brin), Apple (Steve Jobs, Steve Wozniak, and Ronald Wayne), Microsoft (Bill Gates and Paul Allen), and Salesforce (Marc Benioff, Parker Harris, Dave Moellenhoff, and Frank Dominguez). So, based on our experience as cofounders, investing mostly in businesses with cofounders and building relationships with many, many more, we believe starting a company with a cofounder makes sense for most entrepreneurs.

Nonetheless, doing so also comes with challenges. There is the potential for conflict among the founders, the risk of decision paralysis, and the reality of lower equity. And just like marriage, the majority of cofounder partnerships end in divorce.

It's not that marriage or having a cofounder is inherently bad. Rather, the culprit is insufficient work done upfront before saying "I do" and signing the legally binding paperwork. It takes effort, tons of communication, and care to make both continue to work.

Much like my (Mike's) experience with Jonathan, many cofounders come together around an idea and formalize their partnership before they even solidify their business plan. Yet, who you start a business with is much more important than what the business does. It's far easier to change the business model than to change cofounders.

Entrepreneurs inevitably deal with a ton of crap while building a business, so why do so many of them risk doing it with a crappy partner, or even with an incompatible one?

It's easy to get blinded by the emotions that come with a startup's momentum, the excitement about what could be, glorifying how "great" everything will be, much like two people who rush into marriage without really getting to know each other and having meaningful, sometimes difficult talks.

As an entrepreneur, you come up with a great idea (or someone comes to you with a great idea), and you find a potential partner who is ready, willing, and—on the surface, at least—able to help. You dive into it, get going on that business plan, and launch your company.

The emotional highs soon give way to the realities of the work, personalities begin to clash, deadlines are missed, misunderstandings take flight, and your amazing idea stews in a relational toilet that will never improve without a good flush.

Starting a company is an exercise in creativity and ingenuity. It is the process of going from nothing to something and is unique to the human experience. We are hardwired to seek relationships and community. This makes the appeal of a partnership strong. The key is to pick the right partner before saying, "I do."

A MISSHAPED MATRIX

Looking back on what went off course at Shape Matrix, I (Mike) should have known better. I am an experienced serial entrepreneur.

Jonathan is a gifted artist. We should have driven the conversations at the onset to better understand our skill sets, vision, approach to the business, division of labor, and overall compatibility. And we should have spent the time to get the clarity needed to greenlight the venture.

Jonathan and I were friends but far from a good fit as business partners. While I tried to focus the company on core commercial applications, Jonathan was spending most of his time uncovering new and novel ways to apply the technology, even if, at the time, there were no commercial applications—or at least, none we could sell.

As of this writing, the company is still alive, and Jonathan is trying to figure out how to best apply his technology. The eternal optimist in me hopes he succeeds. So if you are interested in killer technology with security, supply chain, and AI applications, call me.

As I have told the investors, I have no hard feelings toward Jonathan. He is brilliant, and his creativity is beyond measure. I have seen his compassion and kindness for more than a dozen years. I have seen him light up inner-city kids, inspiring them to make art they didn't think they could create. He has done the same for my own kids, and they fondly remember those times—sitting on his studio floor with pieces of paper bigger than they were, drawing with giant pieces of graphite and charcoal, and realizing that art can be fun.

Jonathan passes with flying colors if you judge a person by his positive impact on the world. Nonetheless, his position as the majority shareholder of a company in control of the commercial rights to his life's creation made it a conflict between his vision and providing a return for investors, at least in the short term.

After spending three years trying to figure out what I could have done differently to make Shape Matrix a success, I keep coming back to one simple idea: there is no replacement for the missing ingredient from my other successes that were absent from Shape Matrix, and that is a strong cofounder relationship. All of my companies have had great products, unique technology, and strong teams. What I lacked at Shape Matrix was a relationship with an equal business partner built on mutual trust and respect for each other's talents. We ultimately had different visions for the company.

If I had a do-over, I would have explicitly discussed with Jonathan whether we could work together and trust each other. Would he let me do my thing as a successful entrepreneur with multiple profitable exits? Would I be OK with his constant drive to uncover new applications versus focusing on what was known and how to monetize that?

And guess who was skeptical from the beginning? Yes, you got it. Kass! She never told me that I shouldn't go into business with Jonathan. She loved Jonathan and the technology. But her gut was right from the beginning—Jonathan is a sweet guy who could be challenging to work with inside a fast-paced tech-forward environment, especially having never been a cofounder.

When you start a business, you can expect to work seven to ten years with your cofounder, provided things go well. Some form a lifetime partnership, and that's the mentality we think all founders should have going into it. You don't walk down the aisle at your wedding thinking about a divorce. You expect it to last forever.

Of course, business partnerships, unlike most marriages, have an opportunity to end in healthy ways where everyone benefits (financially and otherwise) from their time together. For that to happen, you need to start with confidence that you and your cofounders are simultaneously the same and different.

STARTING ON THE SAME PAGE

We see our partnership as a model for other entrepreneurs, married or not. Many investors didn't see it that way, especially early on, and refused to work with us because we were a husband-wife team. As it turned out, we were right for each other—as a couple and as business partners.

By the time we cofounded Buddy Media, we had worked together to launch our consulting firm (Lazerow Consulting), raised and loved a dog (RIP Cookie), and kept three kids alive. We had pretty much de-risked the cofounder relationship. Most of our work as investors and advisors involves evaluating the fit between the founders. We won't do a deal if we aren't confident in the partnership.

When we reflect on our experiences as founders, investors, board members, and observers of the startup scene, we identified five areas where we think it's essential for partners to reach common ground if they have any chance of shoveling the crap that's in store for them and their new company.

The vision. Founders need to agree on where they want to go. The shared vision seems like the easy part, but, in fact, misalignment can be overlooked if you don't communicate or if you make bad assumptions. Jonathan and I both had a vision for Shape Matrix, but, looking back, it doesn't seem like it was a shared vision.

The values. It's also easy to assume you share values. It's unlikely that you'll find a potential partner who openly claims to lack integrity, for instance, but if honesty is important to you, then you'll want to learn enough about the person to know how likely they are to cut corners that you would never cut.

Other values are less easily classified as "good" or "bad." If your cofounder has three children and an ailing parent and tells you family is a top value, how will that shape his or her commitment to the business? Or will a cofounder who values compassion find it hard to fire employees who aren't doing their part?

Cofounders don't have to have the same core values, but they need to know and respect each other's values and understand how those values will show up in leadership, strategy, and tactics involving the company.

This is essential to developing mutual respect and trust. Because our partnership, like our marriage, is founded on mutual respect and trust, we have never had to worry about whether a promise made would be a promise kept. We assume the best in each other, and that's what we typically get. And when we let each other down in any way (yes, it happens!), the foundation is solid, which makes forgiving, learning lessons, and moving forward all natural responses.

Communication. You can spend a fortune on books and workshops designed to teach effective communication techniques. In our opinion, the point is to apply those techniques when brainstorming ideas, discussing difficult issues, and giving and receiving constructive feedback, not only with each other but also with employees. Brutal honesty (with respect) is a requirement.

Partners unwilling to share their thoughts or consider the ideas of others end up killing the culture and the business because people tend to assume the worst when communication is absent.

Communication is also a critical skill in resolving the inevitable conflicts that arise between cofounders. Research by Noam Wasserman, dean of the Yeshiva University Sy Syms School of Business and author of *The Founder's Dilemmas*, found that 65 percent of startups fail due to founder conflict.[*]

You need a cofounder who can work with you to shovel because how well you get along when things are going well matters far less than how well you get along when the bottom falls out.

If founders have mutual respect and trust and can communicate effectively, they are better equipped to handle disagreements, conflict, and oh-shit moments. If you are considering a partner with a history of avoiding conflict, find a different cofounder.

The mindset. Strong partnerships share a growth mindset, which Carol Dweck, the Stanford professor who popularized the study of this concept, describes as "individuals who believe their talents can be developed (through hard work, good strategies, and input from others)."[†]

Cofounders don't just need to believe this about themselves, but they also need a shared growth mindset about the company. You want your cofounder to have a similar commitment to embracing challenges, pushing through obstacles, learning from constructive criticism, and finding inspiration in the people around them.

---

[*] Nam, Evelyn. "Cofounders Need to Learn How to Productively Disagree." *Harvard Business Review,* December 26, 2022. https://hbr.org/2022/12/cofounders-need-to-learn-how-to-productively-disagree.

[†] Dweck, Carol. "What Having a 'Growth Mindset' Actually Means." *Harvard Business Review,* January 13, 2016. https://hbr.org/2016/01/what-having-a-growth-mindset-actually-means.

A shared commitment to the business idea is important, but the best entrepreneurs, as we will discuss later, recognize that change is a way of life in a startup. The product or service you start with might never take off because the market demands something different. Technologies evolve. Governments rise and fall. Assumptions turn out to be flawed.

A partner with a rigid mindset is like an anchor holding you in shallow water.

The workload. Cofounders must bring an equal commitment to doing what it takes for the company's success. While they can each play roles that cater to their strengths, it can't be a relationship where one partner does 90 percent of the work. That leads to frustration and bitterness for the more committed partners and mixed messages for employees.

COMPLEMENTARY ENTREPRENEURS

We had (and still have) plenty in common, but in marriage and in business, it was our differences—our unique strengths and perspectives, combined with mutual respect and trust—that made us successful. Founders must be like-minded while bringing complementary skills and personalities to the partnership. As Kass often says, your cofounder needs to "fill in your gaps."

Self-awareness is critical because you need to know your strengths to play to your strengths, and you can't be blind to your weaknesses if you expect to find and value partners with strengths you lack.

Working together was a no-brainer for us because our skill sets and personalities are complementary. Mike thinks in screenplays, and Kass thinks in spreadsheets. Mike focuses on ideas, sales, raising money, and the company's strategic direction. Kass handles all business operations, finance, marketing, and human resources—the employees who are always the most important assets to any company.

Kass: "I kind of envision it like a boat. He's at the front looking for land, and I'm trying to get everybody to paddle at the same speed in the right direction."

Because we are aligned on the aforementioned five areas, we can swim in our own lanes while providing the yin to the other's yang. We also had other partners who provided skills that we specifically needed at the time. With Golf.com, for instance, Mike Caspar was essential because he had the talent neither of us had as a developer and technology guru.

We regularly see founders shipwrecked by their similar skill sets. If both are highly operational, they can quickly become paralyzed in the weeds, and neither takes time to look up and determine if what they are offering is actually what their clients want. If both are visionaries, they often drive off a cliff, not understanding the processes they need to put in place to implement their vision.

We've been fortunate to work with several companies that model a complementary approach to cofounders. If you think of Salesforce, for instance, you think of Marc Benioff, but there were four founders: Marc along with Parker Harris, Dave Moellenhoff, and Frank Dominguez.

Marc is the CEO and visionary leader who became the face of the company. He rightly gets the credit for coming up with the idea behind the Cloud software industry. However, Marc quickly points out that he could not have created a $250 billion enterprise without his three cofounders' product and engineering chops.

Frank was one of the initial product developers, writing much of the initial code. Dave focused more on the technical architecture, ensuring their product would scale. And Parker headed up all product development.

Jan Koum and Brian Acton provide another example of complementary cofounders. They became friends while working together at Yahoo, and both applied for jobs at Facebook and were rejected. Then, in 2009, they put together a small team to build WhatsApp, and by the end of 2013, they had four hundred million active users. They sold to Facebook in 2014 for $19 billion! Both came with technical backgrounds, but Brian had more experience in business operations and led the efforts for their early fundraising, while Jan was the technical lead. They had defined and different roles that supported their success.

Getting the cofounder piece right on the front end, as example after example demonstrates, sets up a new company for success. But that's just the first part. Once you have the right partners and you feel passionate about your idea, you still need to look critically and realistically at the business before you leap into the abyss. Only with ample reflection and diligence will you make an informed decision when you reach the critical "go" moment with your business.

CUTTING THROUGH THE CRAP: KEY LESSONS LEARNED

- Starting a business without a cofounder is not always a bad idea, but many of the largest companies in the world usually have two or more founders.

- Choose your partner as carefully as you would your spouse, because who you start a business with is often more important than what the business does to start. It is easier to change business models than cofounders.
- Cofounders must have a shared vision, common values, effective communication, a growth mindset, and an equal workload.
- Self-awareness is critical for entrepreneurs. Know your strengths and weaknesses, and partner with someone whose strengths complement yours and fill in your gaps.

CHECKING THE GO GAUGE
THE CRAP THAT COMES WITH VETTING THE IDEA.

It was April 14, 2011, and our dream of building a large company on the back of the social media revolution was now a reality. Buddy Media had hit its stride and was growing like crazy. We were tired but felt great, and I (Mike) sat at my computer trying to shovel myself out of the crap that was in my email inbox when a message from Walter Driver attracted my attention.

Walter and I knew each other through the tight network of entrepreneurs building on the Facebook developer platform. In his email he wrote that he was raising money for Scopely, a new company developing "social engagement games and applications that help people discover and build relationships with each other online in real time."

I loved the idea. Casual online games back then were mostly single-player. You played against a computer, and any social hooks involved a leaderboard or chat box to talk to other players.

Buddy Media's initial foray on the Facebook platform involved trying to make games social. We were not game developers and pivoted into enterprise software. Walter had taken the social gaming idea much further and attracted two talented cofounders.

Eytan Elbaz, the chief strategy officer, was a founding member of Applied Semantics, which created the AdSense product that Google acquired in 2003 in a nine-figure acquisition that served as the foundation of its massive search monetization business. The company's head of technology, Ankur Bulsara, previously led the engineering team that built the MySpace Developer platform and founded Brainwave Software Consulting.

I spoke to Kass about investing in Scopely. She agreed. And we became part of a group that provided Walter the seed capital Scopely needed to launch.

Walter never sent us a business plan. Instead, he sent us answers to a few simple questions—answers that served as the blueprint and North Star for creating the country's largest independent mobile game company before selling it for about $5 billion in cash in 2023.

We often use Walter as an example of how to decide whether to launch a company. He did the hard work necessary to address the fundamental questions all entrepreneurs need to answer. Without solid answers to these questions, there's no point in talking about funding. These six basic questions form the "Go Gauge," a filter through which we analyze the early-stage deals presented to us:

- **Product:** What are you selling?
- **Differentiation:** Why is it better than existing options?
- **Customer:** Who will buy it, and how many potential customers exist (market size)?

- **Sales and Marketing:** How will customers find out about your product?
- **Delivery:** How will you get it to customers?
- **Financial model:** Does the financial model pass the smell test?

As serial entrepreneurs and early-stage investors who have backed more than 100 startup companies, we have seen thousands of pitches. The ones that resonate clearly (and succinctly) answer these questions.

Business school textbooks, case studies, and the thousands of how-to guides for entrepreneurs often complicate decision-making. The job site Indeed.com, for instance, describes a business plan as a "30-to-50-page document."[*] NerdWallet, meanwhile, recommends nine sections and a series of appendices.[†] The Small Business Administration offers two really simple templates—a traditional format that only takes about eight pages and a "lean startup format" that is one page.[‡]

In our experience, the more complex the plan, the harder it is to get to the purity of vision needed to invest time or money into

---

[*] "9 Steps to Writing a Business Plan (With 2 Templates)." *Indeed,* accessed August 7, 2024. https://www.indeed.com/hire/c/info/business-plan-templates?gad_source=1&gclid=CjwKCAiA0PuuBhBsEiwAS7fsNQkcrX2yVZ23LPVcarv080YP8mRnCDbae4ZLMeGnLniMZTe8fNveIhoCcaYQAvD_BwE&aceid=&gclsrc=aw.ds.

[†] Murphy, Rosalie. "How to Write a Business Plan, Step by Step." *NerdWallet,* June 18, 2024. https://www.nerdwallet.com/article/small-business/business-plan.

[‡] "Write Your Business Plan." *U.S. Small Business Administration,* accessed August 7, 2024. https://www.sba.gov/business-guide/plan-your-business/write-your-business-plan.

an idea. The best companies often start with a simple story that is easy to explain, and that's exactly how Walter responded to the Go Gauge questions.

Product: "*Scopely is building social engagement games.*"

Scopely's product was nothing new: games for the masses. In the last five thousand years thousands of multiplayer games have hit the market, from checkers to chess, Scrabble to Clue, backgammon to Yahtzee, cribbage to Uno!, and mancala to Jenga. Walter identified a new opportunity based on a time-proven premise that the best games are social.

Differentiation: *They "help people discover and build relationships with each other online in real time . . . and the competitive landscape is mostly undeveloped."*

Instead of building another social network, Walter offered games people could play within communities on emerging technologies. Scopely, in other words, allows you to play Yahtzee or Monopoly (two of its biggest games) with your college roommate in Hong Kong while you ride the subway to work in New York. And games like *Star Trek Fleet Command* require players (friends) to join teams with each other. Social activity is not an add-on. It is the foundation.

By the time Scopely launched, several large public—and at least five private—gaming companies were trying to tackle the social game space. Its biggest competitor, Zynga, was started by Buddy Media and Facebook investor Mark Pincus. At the time of Scopely's launch, venture capital investors had invested in Zynga at an $8 billion valuation. Other gaming companies were valued between $400 million (Rock You) and $1.2 billion (Badoo).

Scopely was different for two main reasons—social interaction was at the core of all Scopely games, and those games were built around existing intellectual property like Yahtzee, *The Walking Dead*, and *Star Trek*. The other companies invented new intellectual property, which was expensive and required significantly more capital to market.

Customer: *Online game players.*

Almost everyone enjoys playing games, regardless of age, gender, ethnicity, income, political ideology, or any other demographic or psychographic category. Online gamers in the US are mostly adults (76 percent in 2022 with an average age of thirty-five) and almost equally split between males (52 percent) and females (48 percent).[*]

The market size for these applications was in the "billions of dollars," Walter noted. More than 100 million online game players and half of all entertainment dollars flowed through what's known as interactive entertainment. The market for his product was huge, to say the least. And it was growing. As of 2021, 40 percent of the global population, 3.24 billion people, were gamers.[†]

Sales and marketing: *Scopely games "are built as a layer upon existing communication platforms, such as social networking or mobile."*

The fast-growing social platforms offered direct access to players. The platforms also offered access to the social graph (the connections between you and the people, places, and things you interact

---

[*] Stojanovic, Milica. "Gamer Demographics: 2024 Game-Changing Statistics Worth Checking" *Playtoday,* February 9, 2024. https://playtoday.co/blog/stats/gamer-demographics/.

[†] Stojanovic, Milica. "Gamer Demographics: 2024 Game-Changing Statistics Worth Checking" *Playtoday,* February 9, 2024. https://playtoday.co/blog/stats/gamer-demographics/.

with online[*]), which made it easy for players to invite friends. When you added paid media on top, the social platforms provided one of the world's most efficient forms of word-of-mouth marketing.

Delivery: *Mobile phone app stores (Apple) and social network sites.*

Scopely went to where the users were already hanging out—online. This helped accelerate the company's growth by giving customers familiar and convenient access to its products.

Financial model: *Very profitable unit economics as "products will unlock huge revenue potential from a hybrid subscription and virtual currency model to access premium features."*

While Scopely offers free games, players who want to excel can purchase virtual goods from a virtual store—and the cost to create these goods is nearly zero. These free games are profitable even after an app store takes a 30 percent cut. Selling virtual goods that cost nothing to make is a high-margin business! While less than 5 percent of players spend money on casual games, that's enough to generate significant revenues. Non-purchasers add value by generating ad impressions that can be monetized, as well as by inviting their friends to the game, which lowers the company's customer acquisition costs.

The scale of Walter's $5 billion success was larger than we could have ever imagined when he pitched the idea in April 2011. But with a strong team and the ability to articulate answers to these questions, we were not surprised that he could build a special company with well over $1 billion in annual revenues and still growing!

---

[*] Dickinson, Boonsri. "So What The Heck Is The 'Social Graph' Facebook Keeps Talking About?" *Business Insider,* March 2, 2012. https://www.businessinsider.com/explainer-what-exactly-is-the-social-graph-2012-3.

THE ACCELERATED BUSINESS PLAN

Research by PitchBook found that 3,200 private venture-backed companies in the US went out of business in 2023, taking about $27 billion in investments with them.[*]

Those companies might have gotten some or even all of our questions right on the front end and still failed because there are other factors involved—the execution of the plan, the willingness or unwillingness to pivot when needed, and the unpredictable influences of outside forces like competitors, geopolitics, and the weather, for example. But we're confident that using the Go Gauge would have saved many—perhaps most—a lot of time, money, and heartache.

The best reason to write down your answers to these questions is to prove to yourself that the idea makes sense. If you can't convince yourself, you shouldn't try to convince anyone else that your idea is worth pursuing and investing in.

Entrepreneurs, including the two of us when we launched our first company, typically don't have money when they launch their business. They have dreams and time. While there are no limits to entrepreneurial dreams, time is limited.

Launching a business that makes no sense on paper is likely to burn valuable time you will never get back. Testing your idea on the front end with these questions at least allows you to shelve the idea and/or pivot to a new one.

Whether buying a bunch of laundromats or starting something that's never been done before, you still need to go through this vetting

---

[*] Teo, Kai Xiang. "$27 billion up in smoke – that's how much cash the 3,200 startups that failed this year had raised, says Pitchbook" *Business Insider*, December 7, 2023. https://www.businessinsider.com/failed-venture-capital-startups-burnt-27-billion-pitchbook-2023-12.

process before going forward. You can also work through the Go Gauge with anyone you trust and with potential customers. If the people you expect to buy your product aren't sold on the business or if people you truly trust start trying to talk you off a ledge, then killing the idea is often the best decision you'll ever make.

So, let's take a more detailed look at the Go Gauge and how other entrepreneurs answered its questions.

Product: What are you selling? Nicolas Jammet, Nathaniel Ru, and Jonathan Neman were college students who shared a disappointment in the food options on their campus at Georgetown University.

"There were two choices: food that was slow, expensive, and fresh—or fast, cheap, and unhealthy," they later would say. "We saw an opportunity to create a business where quality was never sacrificed for convenience."[*]

Two months after graduating in 2007, the trio opened Sweetgreen in Washington, DC, and began serving customers. Now, the company has more than two hundred restaurants in nearly twenty states.

They identified their product early on, and, as a bonus, it was something they believed in—healthy food. When it comes to your product, it helps to "eat your own dog food," as the saying goes. That has nothing to do with Sweetgreen, which offers excellent people food. It just means you should use your own products and be the most knowledgeable customer, because if you don't love it and don't know everything about it, why would anyone else care?

---

[*] "Our Mission." *Sweetgreen,* accessed August 7, 2024. https://www.sweetgreen.com/mission.

Differentiation: Why is your product better than existing options? You don't need a perfect product to start a business. Perfection is not possible, nor should it be the goal. As Guy Kawasaki often points out, great companies start with imperfect products and improve them along the way, especially in the tech business (think software version releases!).

However, you do need a product that offers something better than what already exists. Sweetgreen was a quick-serve restaurant with healthy food options. Uber and Lyft were about democratizing access to private car services.

Differentiation can take many forms—faster, cooler, smaller, bigger, cheaper, fancier, and more—and different today can quickly become the same tomorrow as new competitors enter the market.

Some experts recommend evaluating the competition as part of your business plan, and it's certainly good to know who else is in the game. But rarely is a market winner-take-all. If there's a big market, there's almost always room for multiple competitors, so the key is to stand out by offering something different and better than anyone else. Competition is seldom the reason a company fails.

Customer (question 1): Who will buy your product? Even if you have a product that everyone uses, that doesn't mean everyone will buy it from you.

Everybody enjoys games, but Scopely targeted those who play online and would likely find value in playing games with friends. Everybody eats. Sweetgreen targets those who value healthy food options, convenience, and reasonable prices.

Customer (question 2): How many potential customers exist (market size)? Understanding the basics about your core customer helps you answer the related question about market size.

For example, as part of an assignment in an entrepreneurship class, a couple of college students came up with a business idea for a koozie that fits Mickey's Fine Malt Liquor, which at the time had an odd bottle shape with a "big mouth" top. Since they were duck hunters who grew up in Texas, they designed their koozies with a camouflage pattern in the shape of their home state.

So, who would buy their product? Mainly duck-hunting college students from Texas who regularly drink Mickey's Fine Malt Liquor.[*] If they took that answer forward in our Go Gauge, they would discover the market size to be small. That's probably a no-go moment.

The potential number of customers and sales, aka the market, needs to be big enough to support the size of the company you want to build. Large businesses can't be built in small markets, and small businesses can't be built in markets that don't or won't exist. If you are the only option in the market, the market most likely doesn't exist or is too small to support a healthy company.

Save yourself a ton of pain and pick a large market to attack.

The founders of Sweetgreen knew there was a huge market for people who eat out regularly. On average, Americans dine out three times a month and order delivery 4.5 times per month.[†] And three out of five Americans go out for dinner at least once a week.[‡]

---

[*] Zweig, Mark. *Confessions of an Entrepreneur: Simple Wisdom for Starting, Building, and Running a Business.* Epic Books, 2022.

[†] "The Diner Dispatch: 2023 American Dining Habits." *US Foods,* accessed August 7, 2024. https://www.usfoods.com/our-services/business-trends/american-dining-out-habits-2023.html.

[‡] "Eating Out." *Centers for Disease Control and Prevention (CDC),* May 15, 2024. https://www.cdc.gov/diabetes/managing/eat-well/eating-out.html.

The founders also identified a large market of people who preferred healthy food options. This was confirmed when like-minded customers flocked to their first location in DC, which gave them the confidence to quickly expand to multiple cities nationwide. The company was an early leader in the global health and wellness food market and is now worth about $861.1 billion (and growing).*

Sales and marketing: How will customers find out about your product? No one is sitting at home looking for you. "If you build it, they will come" made a great hook for *Field of Dreams*, but it is not a good business strategy. Customers aren't going to find you on their own. They will find you through your marketing and advertising, through a referral from a friend, or by walking in front of your store.

Once you know who your customers are and what matters to them, you need a cost-effective way to reach them. When your efforts fail, you must optimize, evolve, and maybe even pivot to other tactics.

Some companies like Wayfair and Chewy only sell directly to customers online. Smaller retailers and service companies that cater to local markets might only have stores. Walmart, Disney, Starbucks, commercial airlines, and many other large brands take an omnichannel approach, integrating online, mobile, and physical experiences. And others, like software developers on the Salesforce AppExchange or Apple App Store, sell through companies that already have relationships with potential customers. All of these

---

* "Global Health and Wellness Foods Market to Reach $1.6 Trillion by 2030." *GlobeNewswire,* February 16, 2023. https://www.globenewswire.com/news-release/2023/02/16/2610004/0/en/Global-Health-and-Wellness-Foods-Market-to-Reach-1-6-Trillion-by-2030.html.

models can work, but you must decide what will most likely connect your customers to your product.

Delivery: How will you get your product to your customers? If you have a great product that's better than other similar products, a big market for that product, and great ways of telling that market about the product, you still need to deliver that product to the customers.

Sweetgreen has restaurants. Scopely delivers through app stores. How will you deliver your product?

Financial model: How does the financial model pass the smell test? Neither of us was a finance major, nor are we finance wizards. But we quickly learned that a simple financial model makes all the difference in deciding whether a business makes sense. A financial model that doesn't make sense in a spreadsheet (Kass's favorite tool!) will never make sense in the real world.

We are not the people to teach you advanced financial modeling. This is solely about our approach and what we look for as investors today.

There are two components to the model—revenue and expenses. It gets no more basic than that, right? Your revenue is the sum of all money received from customers. The expenses are the sum of all the costs required to make your products (or the cost of goods sold), as well as all the costs associated with running the company—operations (salaries, benefits, rent, travel, etc.), marketing, and other expenses (interest on debt, taxes, etc.).

Before you greenlight the business, it helps to know how much money you can make from each unit sold, often called your unit economics. The difference between the price a customer pays for your product and the cost of creating and delivering it is your gross profit. The gross profit margin is the percentage of money left after paying for the product's costs.

The higher your gross profit margin, the better. Higher-margin businesses have more money available from each sale to pay for expenses (all other costs associated with the company). Whatever is left goes to the bottom line or net profit. Knowing your unit economics is key.

Determining how you will source your product is a key part of figuring out your unit economics. If you launch a coffee company, you need to know who is providing the beans. How much will those beans cost? How will you get them from plants on a farm to perfectly ground java in vacuum-sealed packaging in your warehouses?

If you are Sweetgreen, what does it cost to make one lunch plate with miso-glazed salmon, warm roasted sweet potatoes, slaw, wild rice, honey barbeque sauce, and a squeeze of lime juice? We have no clue. But you can bet the founders of Sweetgreen know the answer.

The unit economics tells you if the cost of producing and selling your product is more or less than you can charge for the product. If it's more, you have arrived at an obvious no-go moment.

Budgeting is one of the most difficult tasks for entrepreneurs, so we have a simple budget spreadsheet at www.shovelingshit.com to get you started.

Many of us are optimists, which translates into a rosy view of revenue and expense projections that underestimate the costs. Be realistic. Err on the side of caution. Even your most conservative financial model will most likely be too optimistic.

A rule of thumb we live by is that it often takes twice as long and twice as much money to do anything worthwhile. It would not be crazy for you to create your financial model, cut the revenue in half, and double the expenses. You are better off using that as your guide and exceeding your projections than falling short and not having the resources to do what you set out to do.

CHASING A PIECE OF THE PIE (MIKE)

Let's bring all these numbers to life by looking at one of the most delicious industries on the planet . . . pizza!

I have long been fascinated with the pizza industry. As I walk between meetings in New York City, I am sure to pass by one or two small retail shops selling pizza by the slice (or whole pie if you so choose). I have no self-control with pizza. So, I stop often to grab a slice. And I think about the beauty of the pizza model.

A pie with $1 or less in ingredients can sell for $28 here in New York City. No wonder there are more than 72,000 pizzerias in the US.[*] Everyone I know (or at least everyone I like) loves pizza. And if we can't grab a fresh pie or slice, we love it so much that we will even heat a frozen one up. Frozen pizza alone in the US is a $6 billion annual market![†]

As I slam down my slice (or two, who am I kidding), I start to think about how I could get a slice of this market. I consider ideas and crunch some numbers, eventually working through the questions in our Go Gauge.

---

[*] "Pizza Restaurants in the US–Number of Businesses." *IBISWorld,* June 1, 2024. https://www.ibisworld.com/industry-statistics/number-of-businesses/pizza-restaurants-united-states/.

[†] "Global Frozen Pizza Market." *Market.US,* November 2023. https://market.us/report/frozen-pizza-market/.

The easiest way, I imagine, would be to buy or open new pizzerias. I think I could get it done for less than $100,000, but to do it right, I've landed on $175,000, which is more realistic. A pizza place in New York City can make about $20,000 a week, assuming a decent location. That translates to about $1 million in annual revenue. At a 20 percent net profit, I'm looking at $200,000 in annual profit, which is less than a year for payback on my investment to buy or open a pizzeria. Not a bad small business, especially if you can scale and open multiple locations.

Of course, the challenge would be standing out in a crowded market. Could I make pizza that tasted better? Could I win with location or price?

If not, maybe there's another way to enter this industry. But the hardest way to make money is by trying to bring new innovations into a market that hasn't changed in a century. It's difficult to get people to change their long-ingrained behaviors, but that's exactly what Zume tried to do.

Founded in California, the company raised $500 million to cook and deliver pizza on moving trucks. It folded in 2023. One reason, according to the company, was technological issues. It couldn't always keep the cheese on the pizzas as the truck rolled down the street! It's no surprise the company was founded in California. Had they asked any of us New Yorkers, we would have said we were perfectly happy with fresh pizza from the corner pizzerias.

Zume was also solving a problem that didn't exist, while another innovative company, aptly named Slice, created a business serving local pizza operators that has produced delicious results.

Ilir Sela's uncle, grandfather, and father all owned pizzerias, and he easily could have started his own business in keeping with that family tradition. Instead, he set out to solve some of the problems that independent pizzeria owners like his family regularly face.

With a passion for pizza matched only by his love of technology, Ilir launched Slice to empower independent pizzerias with a full suite of technology products that let them compete with bigger chains like Domino's and Pizza Hut: online and app-ordering, a website builder, and marketing services.

Slice says its clients include more than 20,000 pizzerias in all fifty states and more than half of the pizza shops in New York City. Its customers have sold more than $1 billion in pizzas through Slice, and its revenue from those sales has surpassed $100 million annually.[*]

With $500 million, Zume should have just bought up a bunch of pizzerias and dominated that market. Or it could have solved a problem for all of those independent owners like Ilir did. We're not bashing Zume or its investors. The outcome speaks for itself, and we know how difficult it is to back away from a dream even when the Go Gauge turns bright red, warning you to stop.

We relate to all the stories we've shared in this chapter. We have started a company with a small outcome (Golf.com), a large outcome (Buddy Media), and one whose outcome so far looks like Zume (Shape Matrix)!

I didn't follow our own advice when Jonathan Cramer and I launched Shape Matrix. We knew there were huge markets in cybersecurity and supply chain industries that might benefit from this innovative technology, but we had no idea what our product was or how we would find customers for that product.

---

[*] Tan, Michael. "Slice." *Contrary Research*, February 23, 2023. https://research.contrary.com/reports/slice.

Much of our initial time *after* starting the company was spent trying to answer those questions. As we already discussed, we could have saved ourselves and our investors money and frustrations by putting more thought into whether we could work together as cofounders. But we also should have done more work upfront on the business model.

THE PRESSURE TO GO

One hallmark of the modern economy is the speed of change, which creates pressure to rush forward when you have an idea you think has legs. Indeed, timing is critical to any startup, and there are legitimate times to run with an idea while still working out the details involved in your Go Gauge analysis.

So, you don't have to have locked-down answers to every question. But you need to know what you know, what you don't know, and how you plan to address the unknowns. Potential investors will ask. Trust us on that one. And if you aren't prepared with good answers, you will never fund the business, or as we say, you will never feed your baby so it can grow.

CUTTING THROUGH THE CRAP: KEY LESSONS LEARNED

- Regardless of the length of your business plan, you must answer key questions in these six "Go Gauge" categories: product, differentiation, customer, sales and marketing, delivery, and financial model.
- Do the analysis to ensure the financial model passes the smell test, including understanding your unit

economics. Remember, you are better off cutting the revenue in half and doubling the expenses!
- Talk to potential customers to make sure they want what you will sell them.
- Doing the initial planning reduces the odds of wasting time, energy, and money on a business with little chance of success. If it doesn't work in a spreadsheet, it won't work in the real world.

FEEDING THE BABY

THE CRAP THAT COMES WITH FUNDING THE BUSINESS.

After our daughter Vivi's birth in May 2007, we focused on two primary objectives: keeping our baby alive while caring for Myles and Cole (five and three years old, respectively), and our eighty-five-pound Bernese Mountain Dog, Brownie; and finalizing the plan to birth Buddy Media.

Every inch of our two-bedroom apartment in New York City's Upper West Side was filled with the supplies to sustain our family zoo. We worked mainly in our bedroom, which we don't recommend to any cofounders, and at a small table in the front living room.

It wasn't the most relaxing time for us, but between day camp drop-offs, dog walks, and baby feedings, we were able to answer most of the Go Gauge questions previously outlined. Only one obstacle stood in the way of making the dream a reality: we needed money—a lot of money.

Facebook's move to open its developer platform to third-party applications represented a fundamental shift in the internet, moving it from a single-player experience to a social one. We wanted to be a part of it and move fast, and we knew it would take more money than we had available in our savings to get Buddy Media started.

We needed our own developers because we had prioritized owning our tech stack. That way, we weren't beholden to a third-party development shop's whims and capacity (and delays). So we asked several early Facebook developers if they would like to partner.

Aryeh Goldsmith said yes but with one caveat: we needed to buy his existing apps—Matches (then the most popular dating app on Facebook) and a few other less popular ones. After much back-and-forth, we agreed to pay $200,000 in cash plus equity in the new Buddy Media business. (Aryeh left Buddy Media for personal reasons after launch, and one of our other investors purchased his stock.)

In addition to the cash for Aryeh, we needed about $1.5 million for the first year to get an office and hire a team of engineers to build out the apps. With three kids and having just purchased our first apartment in New York City, we had plowed through what we'd earned from selling Golf.com, so now we were cash-poor.

Our first call to raise the money was to Howard Lindzon, one of the best early-stage investors we know. We hadn't known each other very long but trusted his instincts and advice. Howard has a great feel for markets, opportunities, and young founders, and was the first investor in several successful companies—Rent.com, Robinhood, eToro, Lifelock, and Manscaped.

Neither Howard nor I (Mike) had an office. So, we met at the Stone Rose Lounge, which overlooked Central Park in the building formerly called the Time Warner Center. It typically drew crowds for cocktails and late-night drinks but was practically empty when we met mid-afternoon on an early summer day in 2007.

I told Howard about our newest venture, and he loved our plan and committed on the spot. While his $50,000 would be a small part of Buddy Media's seed round, we were off and running. The momentum from his commitment and introductions to other investors proved invaluable and helped us close $1.5 million in September from a great group of angel investors.

We announced the company's launch on September 23, 2007, with a plan to develop Facebook's de facto virtual currency: Acebucks. Users could earn Acebucks by installing certain apps and referring their friends. They could spend their digital dollars on virtual goods in our virtual mall or put them toward physical items like an iPod Nano.

The initial plan (and a subsequent plan after that!) did not work, so we successfully pivoted to a software-as-a-service (SaaS) model about eighteen months after our launch. However, we never would have gotten there if we hadn't kept one key priority at the top of our list: feeding the baby.

BUSINESS 101: STAY IN BUSINESS

There's only one way a company goes out of business: it runs out of money. Money is to businesses what food is to babies. No food, no toddler. A company with no revenue can survive as long as it still has money in the bank, but a brilliant plan sans money and you are toast. People don't work without pay.

We tell founders that the first three jobs of an entrepreneur are:

1. Don't run out of money.
2. Don't run out of money.
3. Don't run out of money.

It's a simple concept. But one that many entrepreneurs don't internalize until it's too late. Hoping that revenue grows or that investors will put in more money is not a strategy. Again—because it's a mantra we live by—life as an entrepreneur is easier if you assume your business will take twice as long AND twice as much money to do anything that matters.

Many businesses are profitable from day one. Accountants, lawyers, consultants, and other service businesses, where the entrepreneur is the product, can earn immediate revenue. If you are building a product (manufacturing, software, etc.) or selling others' products (retail store, e-commerce), you most likely will need to raise money. So embrace the crap that is fundraising because that's how you feed the baby.

We understand the fear that comes with asking people you know for money. We didn't like doing it. In the best of circumstances, asking someone for thousands (or millions) of dollars can feel awkward, especially if you are new to it and haven't developed sales and fundraising skills.

Whether you're raising $5,000 (like Mike did for U-Wire) or the $100 million we raised for Buddy Media, you need to find comfort in the fundraising process. Any discomfort is nothing compared to laying people off or shuttering a business.

Fundraising is no different than any other sales process. And the more you believe in your product—i.e., your company and yourself—the better you will be at funding your dreams. Don't ask for money. Offer investors an opportunity. This should be your mentality. Remember, the worst thing that can happen is that a potential investor will say no.

Like most things, raising money gets easier the more you do it. As first-time entrepreneurs with U-Wire and Golf.com, we had no track record, and our network of potential investors was small. The more success we had, the more we learned, and the larger and more robust our network grew, the easier it got to raise the next round. Eventually, potential investors came to us.

STARTING THE STARTUP

The financial model you created using the Go Gauge includes what will become the first order of business once you decide to move forward with your venture: startup costs. It's much easier to predict costs than revenue. So do your best to be realistic with your expenses.

If you are opening a restaurant, you must lease your space, build it out, hire and train people, and buy food. If you are starting a software company, you need some engineers (if you're not an engineer yourself), computers, and time to build the software. If you are starting a moving company, you need trucks, dollies, furniture pads, insurance, and a few workers with strong backs and the ability to interact in helpful ways with customers.

More often than not, founders bear the brunt of these initial expenses. That means the first person you will likely ask to contribute money to the company's coffers is yourself. We never took out loans, but we used much of our combined savings as young adults, about $30,000, to get Golf.com on the first tee box with computers, software licenses, office supplies (printer, paper, ink), an initial travel budget to go pitch to potential customers, the legal costs to incorporate and trademark, the cost of the URL (which was harder and more expensive back then), and the hosting costs of the website, among other things.

For first-time entrepreneurs, funding your venture often means forgoing a salary and working out of an apartment or garage, which worked out pretty well for Google, Apple, Amazon, Microsoft, Dell, Mattel, Amazon, and Walt Disney.

Think through where your startup money comes from before starting your business. And, we will say it again, you will need more than you probably think at the outset. Once you reach your personal limits, where will you get the rest of the money?

LOOKING FOR POTS OF GOLD

Your contributions as a founder also position you to retain a larger share of ownership when negotiating with outside investors for money to grow and scale. By investing what you can early on, you show potential investors that you are sharing in the financial risks and not just investing your time and energy.

Most of the businesses we have started and invested in needed more money than personal savings or initial revenues would provide. So, we had to look to other sources like angel investors (wealthy friends, colleagues, and family members), venture capital firms, and strategic investors. But there are also other sources—lending institutions (like banks) or government and nonprofit grants, for instance.

Grants aren't always mentioned as a form of funding for-profit businesses, but there's a good bit of money out there looking for a home. And unlike loans, grants don't have to be repaid. Non-dilutive capital like this is great if you can find it. Startups doing innovative research should look to government organizations, like the US

National Science Foundation, a federal agency supporting science and engineering efforts in all fifty states. Its America's Seed Fund program invests up to $2 million annually in startups focused on developing technologies.

In addition to government grants (federal, regional, and state), entrepreneurs can look to corporations and foundations for help starting a business. Visa, Walmart, and Nike, for instance, all offer such programs. Foundations typically support specific founder groups like minorities or veterans. Others have a social good mission and provide funds for companies that address their specific area of interest, like the environment.

When you or the business has assets, you might raise money with debt by taking out loans from a bank or institution. While you retain full ownership of the business, you will often be asked to secure the debt personally. We prefer equity because our interests are aligned with our financial partners—we win together with our investors, and we lose together.

If you find yourself with a high-risk, innovation-based company or lack the assets to secure the debt, you will most likely have to give something up to get the amount of money that feeds your baby's growth. That something is ownership (equity) and a bit of your independence. Not only do investors typically have the right to a share of any proceeds from your business's profits or sale of the company, but you now are accountable to these partners because they are sharing in the risks and reaping the rewards.

Friends, colleagues, and family members typically are your first source of equity capital, especially if you are a first-time entrepreneur. Even Jeff Bezos turned to his family for his initial capital. His siblings, Mark and Christina, reportedly each invested $10,000 in brother Jeff's dream of selling books through the Internet. Each stake in Amazon is worth more than $1 billion today.*

In addition to their financial and moral support, your early investors often provide connections with other potential investors. Their network can become your network. But, as you recall from our Golf.com adventure, things don't always work out as planned. You and your investors risk not only money, but relationships, and relationships are far more valuable and often much harder to repair when damaged. That's why it's particularly important to over-communicate about the risks and the timelines related to the business.

Venture capital firms are professional investment firms. They raise money from pension plans, endowments, and high-net-worth individuals. Some VCs look for entrepreneurs they believe will create the next great technology or innovation. Others focus on specific niches, like health care, cybersecurity, sports, or education.

While VCs provide money and strategic advice, they are far more involved in the business than other partners. Not only do you give up ownership and independence, but you risk ending up with unfavorable terms and losing control to your new partners.

Strategic partnerships are a form of equity funding that we believe you should only consider later in your business's lifecycle. This is when key players like distribution partners buy a stake in your company in exchange for a greater or exclusive role.

Done well, strategic partnerships can provide money and improve efficiencies, but locking arms with a partner might also

---

* "Jeff Bezos convinced his siblings to invest $10K each in his online startup called Amazon and now their stake is worth over $1B — 2 ways to get rich outside of the S&P 500" *MoneyWise,* May 3, 2024. https://moneywise.com/investing/alternative-investments/jeff-bezos-family-investment-amazon-hybrid.

dilute your brand or prevent you from working with other potential partners in a competitive marketplace.

One of our last financing rounds for Buddy Media raised about $50 million by working with strategic partners. Since we had shifted to our software-as-a-service model, we weren't just selling to large brands but also to their advertising agencies, and WPP, a holding group that owns some of the largest agencies in the world, was one of those agencies.

By 2010, WPP's founder and CEO, Sir Martin Sorrell, was the most powerful person in advertising. So we were all ears when he and his team, led by current WPP CEO Mark Read and head of corporate development Sheila Spence, approached us with a deal to make us their preferred partner in social marketing. As an incentive for WPP to push the Buddy Media software to its clients, we agreed to a partnership that included an investment in our company. This streamlined and accelerated our work with their 140,000 employees and hundreds of agencies.

We formed a similar strategic partnership with Publicis Groupe, which, ironically, had acquired Leo Burnett, the company that brought Kass to Chicago to work for GiantStep. If we were raising capital from a strategic partner, it was important that we had two so we didn't become known as either the WPP company or the Publicis company. And we were fortunate to get both on board.

PICKING YOUR PARTNERS

No matter who you work with—VCs, friends, family, or even lenders and grant providers—picking your partners should be a deliberate process. You want to ensure a fit which gives you the confidence to navigate the tough times together and share the fruits of your labor. All investors are friendly during the good times. You need partners who will also be there for you in the tough times.

The best way to pick your investors is to find ones who share your values, understand your vision and timeline, offer mutually beneficial terms, and, if you are lucky, provide tangible value to the business you are building.

Some investors primarily contribute money, even if they are equity investors. Your cousin might invest $10,000 and then have almost no involvement in the business other than reading the reports you send. But professional investors like venture capitalists want to get involved and stay apprised of the latest developments. Some might sit on your board, and others act as advisors. These must be voices you trust (that's where the relationship comes in) and who can work for the money they've invested by providing their skills and expertise.

For instance, if you are opening a restaurant, find a few backers who have worked in the food and hospitality industry. If you know the federal government is potentially a key customer, work with investors who have experience dealing with that bureaucracy. Some investors have name recognition that adds credibility to your startup. Others might have expertise in areas such as finance or fundraising.

If you want to build a business that will go public or take ten years to exit, you need investors with an appetite for that timeline and, ideally, experience going public.

Picking the right partners is pretty straightforward when working with individual investors, like friends and family. It's mainly a matter of clear and upfront overcommunication that there is no pressure to invest; they should only invest capital they are willing to lose and expect this investment to be illiquid for many, many years.

Venture capitalists bring a different perspective because investments are their livelihood and they represent other stakeholders. Regardless of how nice they are to you at the start of the relationship, never forget that they negotiate deals for a living. You don't. They have many companies in their portfolio. You have just one, and you're all in. They know the ins and outs of term sheets and the dynamics of founder negotiations. You most likely don't, unless you have raised multiple rounds.

Unless they invest out of their own family office, these investors manage other people's and institutions' money. Their first obligation is to be responsible stewards of their investors' capital. This is not to say that all professional investors will act against the best interests of your company. But when things don't go according to plan, they will act in the best interests of their investor(s), which could include actions that negatively impact you and the business.

Our advice when considering venture capital partners, first and foremost, is to avoid shotgun marriages.

VC firms that see your company as pregnant with potential often will try to get a ring on your finger before you consider marrying someone else, even if they might ultimately leave you alone at the altar. They will try to lock you into a commitment when exploring your dating options is in your best interest.

During one fundraising round for Buddy Media, several VC firms wanted us to sign a term sheet early on that would lock us into an exclusive negotiation period while they did their due diligence and figured out if they really wanted to do the deal.

We prefer clean financing rounds where all interests are aligned. We have avoided complicated terms for the most part and urge you to do the same if you can. Watch out for terms like *participating preferred, harsh ratchets, unusual blocking rights, forced dividends, 2X+ liquidation preferences, guaranteed returns,* and *set exit dates.*

One firm we were interested in asked if we would consider "a participating security with a low threshold for kick-out (2.5x maybe)?" A kick-out? What does that even mean? Thankfully, we had our own VC ace, Roger Ehrenberg, who helped explain the anti-founder verbiage and steered us to more friendly terms. We still don't completely get it, but we know that any kick-out is a bad way to start a relationship (and we ended up not working with that firm).

If given the preference, we would take a lower valuation for simple, clean terms that align everyone's interests around the table. Investors prefer complicated protections to increase their returns and protect them from downside scenarios.

We are often asked about valuation. Specifically, how do you value a young company? The answer is simple: the price of anything is the price someone is willing to pay for it. It's no different than real estate. You may think your house is worth $1 million, but if you only have one offer for $400,000 after a year on the market, then the value of your house in the current market is $400,000.

Many firms complained about Buddy Media's high valuation during each of our fundraises, but we had very little say in it. Markets are efficient and speak for themselves. We had multiple interested parties for each round. The company was in a new white-hot space (social media) and we were posting massive growth. Complaining about our valuation was like complaining about the weather. It was what it was.

ALWAYS RETURN EMAILS

There's really only one time when founders need to think about raising money for their business: right now. You always need to have your mind in fundraising mode.

Most of the time, however, you aren't raising money, you are growing your network of potential investors by building genuine relationships. The best way to build genuine relationships is to show you care for people regardless of whether they can give you anything in return.

Howard Lindzon, who we mentioned earlier as the first outside investor in Buddy Media, vividly illustrated this point. Ironically, I (Mike) didn't immediately put this principle into practice with him, but it paid huge dividends for us once I woke up.

Shortly after Kass and I sold Golf.com in 2006, Howard invested in GolfNow.com, a company that developed technology for managing online tee times. We didn't know Howard, but he knew about our company, so he reached out for advice. Meeting with him would have been an amazing opportunity for me, but we had young kids, I was consulting, and life was a blur. I pretty much ignored him.

If not for Howard's persistence, Kass and I would have missed out on a wonderful friendship with him and his wife, Ellen, and Buddy Media would have gone without a key figure in its early funding. But persist he did, and after several emails and calls, I eventually agreed to meet with him.

Our relationship quickly took off. He's a great human being with a wicked sense of humor (Kass frequently belly-laughs when around him), and I enjoyed spending time with him.

I told him what I would do about growing an internet business in the golf industry and made introductions that helped him sell GolfNow.com to Comcast, but I never had any quid pro quo in mind. He was just a new friend who needed help I could give, so I was giving it (after I finally returned his emails!). And he owed me nothing a year later when we met at Stone Rose in the summer of 2007. But he provided far more than his $50,000 investment in Buddy Media.

Much of our initial startup funding came from preexisting relationships—family and friends like my brother (John Lazerow), and Keith Bank and Bill Weaver, who knew us, believed in us, and had benefited by investing in Golf.com. But a good bit also came from our connections through newer friends and investors like Howard.

Howard introduced me to Mark Pincus, the founder and CEO of Zynga. Mark was doing what we wanted to do—building on the Facebook platform. Mark and I met over smoothies one day and he loved our idea. He then introduced me to Peter Thiel, an early investor in Facebook who was on Facebook's board. Peter also liked what we were planning, and, as you might expect, having a Facebook board member on our side proved extremely helpful in building a business on Facebook's platform.

After Mark and Peter committed to investing in our company, I sent Howard a thank-you note on July 3, 2007. His response (from his Verizon Blackberry): "Always return emails :)"

Lesson learned.

Howard also introduced us to Roger Ehrenberg of IA Ventures, who became an investor, and James Altucher, a writer who invested in Buddy Media and helped promote the business. They are still friends today. Roger, in turn, introduced us to Karin

Klein, Eric Hippeau, and Jordy Levy (all at SoftBank at the time), and many others.

Throughout the company's history, we raised about $100 million, much coming directly or indirectly from relationships we developed long before it was time to raise money.

I met Jules Maltz, for instance, when he was a student at Stanford. He already had a social advertising company to his credit. After he joined Institutional Venture Partners (IVP) as an entry-level associate, he attended a Buddy Media party we threw at our friend Marc Glosserman's barbeque joint, Hill Country, in New York. Jules and I continued to stay in touch even though we weren't officially raising more funds.

We built a genuine relationship. We trusted him and IVP, and he was helpful whenever I called him. Unlike some other firms, I knew he wasn't talking to our competitors or mining us for information they could use if they invested elsewhere.

In 2010, we raised a $20 million series C financing round from IVP to supercharge our growth even though IVP's proposed valuation was 10 percent less than our other options. The terms with IVP were simple and friendly, which was in line with what we had come to expect from Jules. We liked that we could get in at the beginning of a large fund they were starting, that they had a great reputation with other CEOs we knew, and that they had a track record of backing winners.

We raised money from our friends at Insight Partners (led by Deven Parekh) and GGV Capital (led by Glenn Solomon and Jeff Richards) for our series D financing. By the time each of them invested, they knew the company, and we knew them because we had built relationships even when we didn't need money.

How did we do this? We kept them in the loop. We would send them quarterly updates on our business—our big hires, our new customers, and the events we were hosting. And we'd learn about their interests and look for ways we could add value to their world.

We wanted them to view our company like a nightclub with a long line of people trying to get in—even if you don't know what's happening inside, you figure it's something interesting and worthwhile. If we liked each other, they would jump to the front of the line when opportunities arose to work together, and we could negotiate with a relational foundation, not just from a transactional perspective.

When you are raising money, it's important to focus on the things you can control, like the way you treat people, the investors you will work with, the terms that benefit your business, and how you will use the money. After all, raising money isn't an end in and of itself. It's a means to an end. It's how you feed your baby so it can grow strong and healthy. And putting food on the table is just the beginning. Once you do that, you have something ready to crawl, walk, and run, run, run. Now the real work begins.

CUTTING THROUGH THE CRAP: KEY LESSONS LEARNED

- The number one job of an entrepreneur is to never run out of money.
- You will most likely have to fund the initial startup costs when you launch your company.

- Launching your company with money you have saved puts you in a better position to retain a larger share of ownership later if you raise outside capital.
- There are several choices for raising outside money, including wealthy friends, colleagues, family members, venture capital firms, government and nonprofit grants, and strategic investors. Understand the pros and cons of each (ownership and independence being two of the biggest).
- Be deliberate when picking investors. Look for partners who add value by working alongside you with specific skills and expertise in specific areas. And make sure your timeline, values, and vision match their expectations.
- Avoid a shotgun marriage. If you feel forced into a partnership, it seldom ends well.
- Never stop networking. The relationships you create today could fund your business later.

SITTING AND SHOVELING

HYPER-FOCUSING ON THE RIGHT CRAP ONCE YOU START THE BUSINESS.

A wide-eyed Stanford MBA student wrote a thesis in the 1950s arguing that Americans' interest in fitness would drastically expand the market for athletic shoes. He believed there was an opportunity for a startup business selling shoes to mass-market customers rather than just the competitive athletes targeted by companies at the time.

Phil Knight turned out to be correct. But before Nike was Nike, Knight needed to determine what to focus on and how to get started. As he recalled many years later in his autobiography, *Shoe Dog*, the path was unclear.

After graduating college, Knight traveled to Japan and discovered Tiger running shoes (now ASICS). A runner himself, Knight loved the quality of the shoes. More importantly, the shoes were low-cost for his nascent company, Blue Ribbon Sports—before it became Nike. He convinced the head of Tiger to meet with him and soon locked down the exclusive right to sell their shoes in the western United States. He was off and running.

Before Nike could reach the $50 billion annual revenue it generates today, Knight had to generate the first $1 million. He did it by hyper-focusing on his most important task: selling shoes. He started selling shoes out of the back of his car at track events in the Pacific Northwest and grew the business from there. Without selling those initial shoes, Nike would never have been able to expand into manufacturing its own shoes.

We have seen it over and over again—both with our companies and the hundreds we have seen grow from the seed stage. Hyper-focusing from the start is critical to long-term success.

No one is more focused than our friend Gary Vaynerchuk.

Before Gary was a well-known entrepreneur, social media innovator, and best-selling author, he had huge aspirations and no money. Born in Belarus (the former Soviet Union), Gary moved to the United States in 1978 with his immigrant parents. By age fourteen he was working in his father's neighborhood liquor store, Shoppers Discount Liquors in New Jersey, and in 1996, while still in college, he launched one of the first e-commerce platforms focused on alcohol sales.

After college, in 1998, Gary changed the store's name to Wine Library, and grew it from $3 million in annual revenues to $60 million on the back of his daily video blog series on YouTube called WineLibraryTV. His unconventional and often irreverent commentaries on wine (and the New York Jets) became extremely popular, attracting more than 80,000 viewers daily.

The online videos led to appearances on the Ellen DeGeneres and Conan O'Brien television shows, where he developed a cult-like following. He once smelled O'Brien's armpit to "expand his knowledge" of odors for use when describing wines, demonstrated how a twenty-dollar boxed merlot pairs with hot dogs, and used terms like "sniffy sniff."

Gary was a success by every measure. Well, almost every measure.

While Gary had built Wine Library into a behemoth, he had not created any meaningful financial value for himself. He was thirty-four years old, had never made more than $100,000 in any year, and had zero equity in his dad's company. But he was hungry and full of a pioneer's ambition.

Gary had what Phil Knight called the "crazy idea"—that a new industry would develop on the back of companies interested in using digital content and social media to grow their businesses. And, like Knight, he needed to figure out how to get started when he had no money.

Gary and his cofounder, his younger brother AJ, did all the pre-work we've discussed so far in the Go Gauge. They defined their offering and how they would be different as a digital-first content advertising and marketing service, researched their customers and the market size, knew how they would reach those customers and deliver their services, and built out their financial model.

Part of that model included launching the agency without outside investors, a decision that limited their options (read: cash!) for office space. That led to a call from Gary in 2009 asking if he could take over Buddy Media's conference room to launch VaynerMedia. This was a bold request (something Gary is known for!). He wasn't asking to use the space for a meeting or a day. He wanted our only conference room as his full-time office until his company generated enough revenue to afford a place in the expensive New York real estate market.

Anyone who knows Gary will agree that it is hard to say no to him.

On May 21, 2009, I (Mike) emailed Gary: "You are welcome to come into the office tomorrow. The space is yours. We'll get you set up with keys, alarm, internet, phone, etc. You can have the conference room we discussed. If you need another desk or two, not a problem. You can have full access to the kitchen, pong, etc. You can have the office until we need it back. I'll give you 30-60-day notice for sure if we need it but we're all set for the foreseeable future. I agree with you that being in close proximity will help us work well together."

We witnessed the construction of a global conglomerate up close and have worked closely with Gary ever since. Gary now employs thousands of people, and his businesses include not only a full-service ad agency, VaynerMedia, but a commerce-focused consultancy, a production company, a speakers' bureau, his Veefriends community, and his professional pickleball team, the New Jersey 5s, of which we are minority owners. He has also written seven books, including a children's book, and has been on *The New York Times* bestseller list five times.

Just like Knight's success began by focusing on selling his shoes, Gary started out by hyper-focusing on the first iteration of his business—the social media agency. The rest came on the back of his many successes.

The Bureau of Labor Statistics reports that 20 percent of small businesses fail within the first year, and 30 percent don't make it past their second birthday.* Many don't make it because they hit "go" when the Go Gauge tells them to stop, but others simply fail to focus on the crap that needs to be shoveled first.

If there's one thing all parents know, it's that you deal with a lot of crap in that first year! And the same is true when birthing a business. But too many entrepreneurs don't prioritize what they need to do when they start, do the wrong things, or try to do so many different things that they do few of them well.

That's not Gary's story, and with the right planning and focus, it doesn't have to be yours.

RETURN TO THE REVENUE

You put together a financial model with revenue goals and expense projections for a reason—the process forces you to put in writing a plan against which you can gauge your progress. Without a plan, you will never get where you want to go and never know what success looks like. A plan demands that you decide which priorities are critical and how much time and resources you think it will take to complete them. It also forces you to sideline all efforts that are not top priority.

The goal of the plan is not perfection. As Amazon's founder Jeff Bezos says, any plan "won't survive its first encounter with reality. The reality will always be different."† The goal is to show

---

* "Survival of private sector establishments by opening year." *U.S. Bureau of Labor Statistics,* accessed March 13, 2024. https://www.bls.gov/bdm/us_age_naics_00_table7.txt.

† Bezos, Jeff. *Invent & Wander: The Collected Writings of Jeff Bezos.* Harvard Business Review Press, 2020.

you, after you start executing it, whether you are making the progress you expect.

Entrepreneurs are often quick to point to any positive development as proof they are crushing it. The gap between the story and reality is often enormous. The plan you put together serves as an objective benchmark for showing which of your projections, a.k.a. informed guesses, are *really* working and which are not. This is especially important during your initial year when you have very little data, and your fight to stay in business is fierce.

Imagine you have a gallon jug, and you need to fill it with a certain amount of sand, pebbles, and big rocks. How do you go about it? If you start with the sand and pebbles, you won't get all the big rocks in the jug. But if you start with the big rocks and then fill in with the pebbles and sand, you will maximize the space.

We have always considered the big rocks as organizational priorities. These are the most important tasks at hand, the things that should take most of your bandwidth as an entrepreneur. They aren't the same for every company and can change over time. But whatever they are—sales, hiring, expanding to new markets, etc.—they should be visible and clear to you and everyone in your organization.

The pebbles may not be priorities today. But they matter—or will matter in the next twelve months. Some of our early pebbles at Buddy Media included meeting with potential investors to build important relationships that paid off later, having breakfast with potential future employees, and brainstorming product extensions that led to revenue down the road. These all mattered and produced results. None were critical during Buddy Media's first few months.

Sand is all the small stuff that doesn't differentiate your business but needs to get done. It is the filler that keeps the rocks and pebbles in order. Sand is paying payroll, closing the financials each month, quarter, and year, and filing taxes. A company just isn't a company without sand.

Many tools and frameworks are available to drive an effective planning process. Whatever you use, write it down! If it isn't written down somewhere and available to everyone in your organization, it doesn't exist.

We didn't use a specific planning tool at any of our companies, but we have grown to love Marc Benioff's V2MOM as a simple and effective framework that forces you to make key decisions about your plans and goals. It easily fits on one piece of paper, and it is just as powerful for a one-person startup as it is for a 70,000-person organization like Salesforce.

You can find a sample of the V2MOM[*] on our website, www.shovelingshit.com. It has five compact sections:

Vision: What do you want to achieve?

Values: What's important to you?

Methods: What do you need to do to achieve your vision?

Obstacles: What could get in between you and your vision?

Metrics: How do you measure success for each of your methods?

To figure out what to shovel first, you have to write down in very specific language the two or three big-rock priorities with the

---

[*] If you'd like to learn more about V2MOM, Marc wrote a great article about it in 2020. Here's a link:https://www.salesforce.com/blog/how-to-create-alignment-within-your-company/.

actions and steps you need to take to get the job done in those initial days, weeks, and months.

As Gary once put it, "You have to make sure your actions can respond to the bleeding of cash that occurs before you even turn a profit."[*]

For Gary, it mostly came down to two big-rock priorities:

One: land customers.

Two: hire team members.

Those weren't the only priorities, but those were two of the biggest that he and his team absolutely had to take action on if they had any hope of making it to year two. They had to identify and sell their expertise and services to the businesses that wanted to hire their newly formed team to help with advertising, marketing, and content creation on sites like Facebook and YouTube. And, as a service business, they needed qualified people to do the work they were promising.

The budget projections and assumptions told them how many customers they needed to fund their expenses and provided a forecast for how many people they needed to do the work. And even though it's rare for startups to hit their projections in the first few months (let alone in a year), the financials provide much-needed structure for making progress in the right direction.

The financial plan typically makes the big-rock priorities clear. Tools like the V2MOM, McKinsey's 7-S framework, the balanced scorecard (BSC) approach, or the SWOT matrix, made popular by Stanford and Harvard Business School faculty, all do

---

[*] Vaynerchuk, Gary. "My Advice for First-Time Entrepreneurs…" *Facebook*, March 10, 2017. https://www.facebook.com/gary/photos/a.357303763349/10155073925328350/?type=3.

essentially the same thing. They force you to break down the large, hairy goal into smaller, specific goals, each with its own detailed actions.

In VaynerMedia's newly formed company, Gary and his small team had to determine the division of labor among the six of them. Who was responsible for each goal? Who pitched and sold? Who followed up with a proposal of services? Who was going to provide the services and manage the account, and what did that entail? What other expertise did they need to fill in the gaps?

VaynerMedia quickly grew, and within three months, the company had the resources to move out on its own. None of VaynerMedia's eventual success—let alone moving out of our office—would have happened if Gary had not hyper-focused the team's effort on first-year big-rock priorities: the things that really mattered while sitting in (and shoveling) the crap that comes with growing a business. At the top of his list was landing customers followed by hiring great people who could do the work.

VaynerMedia and Buddy Media's priorities were very different. However, we had the same commitment to hyper-focusing efforts on a core financial and operating plan.

At Buddy Media, we were not able to sell immediately. Instead, our initial plan focused on product development. This is the path for most software companies. It's hard to sell software that isn't built! Our first two large rocks were attracting developers and raising money to cover operational expenses.

With the plan in hand, we aggressively moved both rocks forward. By simultaneously purchasing existing apps and their developers and raising money in record time, we set off with our goal to build Acebucks as a Facebook gaming currency.

We were far from having a perfect product, but we didn't let that slow us down. We are big believers in the time-tested idea of never letting perfection stand in the way of progress, or, as Guy Kawasaki famously puts it in perfect shit-shoveling language: "Don't worry, be crappy."* Be OK with releasing an imperfect product so you can build revenue, a client base, and market share. Then, listen to your customer feedback and keep improving. Too many entrepreneurs are constipated perfectionists—they never launch anything.

By the time we incorporated and launched in September 2007, we had workable but imperfect products, and Mike and Jeff Ragovin (our head of sales), were aggressively selling. This was now one of our big-rock priorities: getting clients. Other big rocks included finding our office space and creating our financial and HR processes. We knew we would be moving fast and wanted to build a solid foundation on which we could grow.

THE CRAP IN YOUR GOALS

Over time, we learned about all the crap you will face once you put your plan in motion.

The number one enemy of the planning process is unattainable goals, especially in the first year. Attainable goals need to be specific, relevant, and time-bound. If you doubt they are realistic, they probably aren't realistic. So, double the time it takes to achieve them or scale them back. As the old saying goes, hope is not a strategy.

---

* Kawasaki, Guy. "The Art of Innovation." *Guy Kawasaki*, accessed August 7, 2024. https://guykawasaki.com/the_art_of_inno/. KaikoMedia. "Guy Kawasaki's TED Talk: 'Don't Worry, Be Crappy'–The Art of Imperfect Innovation" *YouTube video,* 0:59. June 3, 2023. https://youtu.be/vzcV555lY9Y?si=CAM7AyACm3TLD2RX.

A goal is not a goal without a simple, easy-to-understand metric that defines success.

Every rock you prioritize needs a metric that will tell you if you succeeded.

If sales are the number one goal, how do you know if you're doing well? Is it one new customer a week or three or five? (Hint: your budget should tell you that answer.)

If you're going to hire people, how many, what type of people, and by when?

If you want to market, how will you measure the success of that marketing?

If you're focused on operations, how will you measure the success of that team? By seeing that specific tasks are accomplished on time? Or something else?

The metrics will tell you if you are progressing toward, floundering, or overshooting the financial projections you created for that first year. Measurable metrics can also tell you whether you have enough resources to build and support your product or if you should double down on product offerings when revenues aren't hitting targets, or explore options for pivoting to something else.

When putting together your goals, it's also important to consider your potential obstacles.

For instance, many processes took longer while building Golf. com than they did later in our careers. We had no track record of hiring, finding an office space with our limited (no) credit score, or connections with the sites that would likely be interested in syndicating our content. Many of these obstacles melted away with Buddy Media.

We overcame the hiring obstacle at Golf.com by starting lean and turning to people we knew. Our first two employees were Analis Rudy, who had worked with Kass at GiantStep, and Elena Caspar, who was married to Mike Caspar, our cofounder. We convinced our landlord to rent the office space by taking the second floor above it, which is where we lived for a year. Meanwhile, we were able to expand our network with potential customers mainly because of Mike's persistence and the contacts made during his time at U-Wire.

With Buddy Media, we were better at hiring, but the market for engineers was extremely tight and we struggled to compete with larger salaries and equity grants being offered by Silicon Valley startups.

One theme you might have noticed is that hiring the right team is typically a priority for a startup, and it almost always includes obstacles. That's part of the crap that comes with drafting the right team, a topic so important it warrants a chapter unto itself.

CUTTING THROUGH THE CRAP: KEY LESSONS LEARNED

- Your financial model and revenue goals are your initial map of what crap to focus on once you actually start your company.
- From your financial model, identify your big-rock priorities that are critical to getting you to year two and write them down. If you don't write them down, they don't exist.
- FOCUS, FOCUS, and then FOCUS SOME MORE.

- Don't let perfection get in the way of progress with your product or service. Ship imperfect products and improve them along the way.
- Create measurable metrics that will allow you to gauge if you were successful on each big-rock priority.
- Identify as many obstacles to success as possible before you start and immediately work on ways to get over, around, or through them.

MONEYBALLING YOUR TEAM
THE CRAP THAT COMES WITH HIRING FAST AND FIRING FASTER.

It was time to scale, and we knew it.

Buddy Media could only grow fast as an enterprise software company if we had the sales, support, and operations team to handle the growth. By onboarding more sales and client support staff in late 2010 and early 2011, we increased sales to $41.5 million, a 210 percent increase from $13.3 million in 2010. Our team had already doubled in 2011 to 219 employees, and we had plans to grow to about 350 by the end of 2012 with an ambitious plan of doubling our sales.

Customers like Ford Motor Company, Procter & Gamble, L'Oréal, Unilever, Microsoft, Disney, Shell, HP, Visa, and Starwood drove our growth by shifting their marketing dollars away from traditional media (television, print, outdoor) to social media. Almost every large marketer (nine of the top ten global advertisers!) was using Buddy Media's software to manage not only their

Facebook presences and ads but also broader social media marketing on Twitter, YouTube, and Instagram.

These customers were global. Social media was global. Buddy Media needed to go global.

This meant more offices. Our real estate footprint in 2011 included space in San Francisco and a full floor and a half by New York's Penn Station. I (Kass) had just opened our office in London, our gateway to Europe, and Mike was fresh off a trip to the new office in Singapore that would serve our clients in Asia, where social media and mobile penetration was among the highest in the world.

To fund our global expansion, we turned to two of our investors, Glenn Solomon and Jeff Richards from GGV, a leading venture capital firm in Silicon Valley. Glenn was a former NCAA tennis player like me, and Jeff was a recovering entrepreneur with the scars to prove it. We had built a nice relationship with them and were thrilled that they led our $54 million series D financing in August 2011.

We were still learning on the job, but the business was growing fast and had a clear line to hundreds of millions of dollars of revenue. However, we were paying a high price for the company's growth and the required never-ending work. We both had all but stopped working out. Client dinners or "eating at the office" (read: unhealthy snacks or ordering in) and non-stop travel were taking their toll. Our long-standing tradition of Wednesday date nights had faded away, replaced with returning emails and phone calls late into the night after the kids were asleep.

I (Kass) was exhausted when Mike decided we needed a rest from the shit-shoveling chaos.

Mike: "We need a date night."

Kass: "No way, I can't. I'm so tired. I have so much to do, and I'll have to go back and work after."

Mike: "We need to. Let's do it."

Kass: "Where?"

Mike: "Let's see a movie—*Moneyball*."

Kass: "I can't, that will take way too much time. I'm only going if it's really good."

Mike: "You're gonna love it. It's uplifting. It's like *Field of Dreams* and *The Natural*. It's like *Hoosiers*."

Kass: "OK, fine. I'll go."

We asked our sitter to stay later than normal and headed to the theater.

Moneyball appealed to my love for data, statistics, and operational management. It's based on how Oakland A's General Manager Billy Beane changed professional baseball in 2002 by using computer-based analytics to build a championship team on a tight budget. With the help of Peter Brand (the fictionalized version of Beane's real assistant GM Paul DePodesta), the A's found undervalued players whose strengths, when used correctly, combined to form a winning team.

Plus, it starred Brad Pitt, so what's not to love?

I really loved the movie. But it was not the uplifting experience Mike had predicted.

Mike (walking out of the movie): "Wasn't that great!?"

Kass: (no words, just tears starting to well up)

Mike: "What's wrong?"

Kass: "Are you kidding me? Don't you get it? I have to fire two people. And have to totally change two of our teams. I have so much to do!"

Mike: "What are you talking about?"

Kass: "Mike, it was the whole point of the movie—moneyballing. We need to moneyball better. I need to moneyball better."

Even a good movie couldn't take my mind off work; it was just the opposite.

Maybe you learned about moneyballing from Brad Pitt (or Billy Beane). I learned about it from Ralph Savarese. My dad taught me the importance of getting the right people on your team and fielding them in their optimal positions, and that concept would become a core principle in our approach to drafting and building our teams, especially as we scaled.

My dad played basketball at Iona University, so he knew the game and how to put together and manage a team. When I was nine, for instance, he and Amy Hoffheimer's dad partnered as coaches for our youth team. Amy and I were both better-than-average players, so by co-coaching the team, our fathers guaranteed that we had two pretty good players. The other players' talents, to put it kindly, were underdeveloped. But Dad did a masterful job of understanding their skills and using them to complement me and Amy in ways that helped us win games.

I remember sitting down one day as a teenager and asking how he knew where to put everyone.

"Well, you just have to figure out their strengths and play to their strengths," he told me. "Remember that player, Julie?[*] She only ran with her arm out on the right side, so she could never defend someone to her left. That's why I put her at the top right point."

---

[*] Not her real name.

This was my first moneyball moment. Watching the movie years later with Mike reminded me that I needed to put even more of my moneyball principles into practice, even if it wouldn't be easy.

And it wasn't easy. But it was the best way for us to grow, scale, and win.

THE FIRST MONEYBALL STAGE

All great entrepreneurs know a little secret: hiring employees isn't a task on your to-do list. It's the lifeblood of your company. It *is* your company.

The first twenty employees are important. They become the soul of your business. They set the tone for all future hires. If they are awesome, other awesome people will follow, especially when you incentivize them to recruit great coworkers. If they suck, and some will, then you better deal with that quickly, or their suckiness will spread like an infection.

Moneyballing in this stage involves figuring out the roles you need to fill, hiring the right people (including cultural fit, covered in the next chapter), adjusting your teams as the company changes so all the players are in the right positions for success, and firing those who do not succeed in their roles.

In the early stages of a company's life, founders typically do many things simply because there's no one else to do them. You aren't just leading and managing sales (Mike), operations (Kass), HR (Kass), product development (Mike), fundraising (Mike), or accounting (Kass); in many cases, you are also doing the actual work.

You own the bakery and you make the pies. But there are usually things founders can't do (because they lack the skills) or shouldn't do (because that's not the best use of their time). Neither Mike nor I were coders or attorneys, for instance.

The initial hires fill these gaps in ways that are directly tied to your big-rock priorities and financial metrics. For some companies, the first hires are software engineers, for others, they're a salesperson or two, a client manager, a chef, or a delivery driver.

At Buddy Media, we based our hiring strategy on the needs of our customers.

Our initial business model involved building apps, which required specific technical skills. We had the apps we bought from Aryeh Goldsmith, but these needed further development, and we knew we would need new apps as well, so we prioritized hiring engineers.

Our most important technical hire was Patrick Stokes, a young, whip-smart engineer with a biting sense of humor who had built websites for nursing homes and other clients since attending Marist College a few years earlier. Like Aryeh, Patrick had built several popular Facebook apps on the side, including his own dating app (called Crushes), all of which we acquired as part of his hire.

Patrick was young. But we knew he could grow as an engineer and as a leader. He went on to lead our tech team through the Salesforce acquisition in 2012 and has since thrived at Salesforce, where he serves as an executive vice president and has helped build some of the company's most widely used products.

We also needed strong utility players. In moneyball terms, we didn't need players who only hit home runs or struck out. We needed players who could field any position, get on base, and advance runners when needed.

We needed people like the multi-talented Abby Lauterbach.

Abby is now a superstar sales executive at LinkedIn. But when we met her through Mike's brother Robert, Abby had just graduated from New York University. She had the skills of a Swiss Army knife and a willingness to wear every hat in the haberdashery. She was creative (you should have seen her Lite-Brite installation for her final project at NYU), a whiz at PowerPoint and Photoshop, responsible beyond her years, incredibly funny, and shared our values.

Every startup needs an Abby early on—an all-around player to support sales efforts with presentations, respond to clients' needs, and help founders with internal operations and hiring.

Another early addition was Katherine Bateman (affectionately known as KB) of Kayelbee Associates, the best brand marketer in the business. If we were to succeed, we needed to get our name out there and appear as the leader. That meant having the right brand strategy, brand identity, brand messaging, sales materials, and so on (more on marketing in Chapter 11) so that our brand could withstand any potential pivots we would need to make.

KB became more than just a consultant. She was our partner. She rolled up her sleeves and got her hands dirty doing everything from our brand marketing to grunt work like stuffing mailers and negotiating for events and speaker opportunities. She is the exact type of outside vendor you need to partner with, especially with a limited marketing budget.

For the actual sales—a big-rock priority for Buddy Media in year one—we had Mike, but needed someone else to own that part of the business because Mike was also responsible for product development, thought-leadership, investor relations, and future fundraising.

Mike emailed everyone in his network, and Anne Sullivan, who headed fundraising for Northwestern's journalism school at that time, forwarded it to Jeff Ragovin. Mike scheduled a meeting on October 1, 2007, at the Starbucks on 29th and Park Avenue.

"I'll be the dashingly handsome one . . . blue shirt, white stripes, and blazer," Jeff wrote Mike when confirming the meeting.

"I'm the ugly one . . . sneakers, jeans, and blue shirt," Mike replied.

Mike was blown away by Jeff's energy, but I wasn't keen on interviewing him. I was annoyed. I had other things to do, and I had dealt with so many salespeople in my life that I couldn't imagine that Mike had found someone worth hiring. Boy was I wrong.

When Jeff came in for his interview, I was on the floor in our new office putting together IKEA desks with my three-month-old daughter Viv asleep in her pram. Jeff walked in with a great vibe. He had and still has such a positive and friendly demeanor. He drew me in so fast with his engaging personality and sincerity that it was hard to ignore him (and I was trying to because I was busy).

He talked about his network, previous experience, and yadda yadda. About ten minutes into the conversation, I snapped out of the spell he cast and asked him with a drill in my hand, "Listen, I've hired and fired hundreds of salespeople. What makes you any different?"

He paused and smiled.

"OK, I'll prove it to you," he said. "On my first day of work, I will bring you a signed deal."

"Yeah, sure," I said.

We shook hands, he left, and I went back to building desks.

As you can tell, I wasn't entirely sold on hiring another salesperson. But I did feel like Jeff had something different. It was Jeff's follow-up email—the best follow-up email from a salesperson I had ever received after an interview—that sold me on him.

Dear Mike and Kass,

It was great meeting this afternoon. I'm even more excited about this opportunity than I was before. I love a good challenge, and I think this is truly an incredible project to be a part of. I'm convinced that this is the next big wave to ride. I know I've got the experience and sales know-how in this field, and I'm confident I'm the guy for you to grow revenue for Buddy Media. I've already got a solid set of ideas, and this is just scratching the surface. I'm ready to mobilize.

With my proven close experience and contacts in the online industry, I can hit the ground running and know you won't find anyone with more motivation and drive than me. (maybe Michael)

Here's what I can bring to the table:

- *Highest level of strategic thinking*
- *Sales know-how*
- *Solid industry relationships*
- *Drive and motivation*
- *Belief in social media as the next big model*
- *Daily weather forecasts*
- *Consistently exceed expectations*
- *Fun guy to have around*

I am looking forward to hearing from you shortly. I know we can make a brilliant team.

Btw Kass: Tomorrow will be partly cloudy, warm, some morning fog, high 85.
8 a.m. temp around ~67

Thanks Again,
Jeff

During the first part of our interview, Jeff asked questions about me—not just about my role and experience but also about my hobbies, likes, and dislikes. He found out that I loved all things weather-related. I found out that he had studied meteorology in college. He paid attention and connected to those details with me on a human level, and not only by (brilliantly) referencing the forecast in his follow-up email. For the next decade-plus, Jeff regularly sent me weather updates, from warnings about a coming snowstorm to a quick heads-up about an approaching rain shower.

In typical Jeff fashion, he also over-delivered with his actual work performance. In fact, he walked in on his first day with two signed deals. Who does that?! And he turned out to be the best salesperson we have ever met, the best hire we ever made, and one of the greatest humans we know.

When we met Jeff he wasn't someone you might normally categorize as a potential superstar. He graduated from the State University of New York at Oswego and had several jobs, mostly working for companies that weren't well-known. But Jeff had *it*, whatever *it* was. He was electric. He was driven. He had grit, tenacity, empathy, and unbelievably high EQ. He was everything we needed.

When true superstars appear at your doorstep, open up and invite them in because their value to your business will far exceed the cost of employing them. Jeff's impact on Buddy Media was so significant that in 2012 we named him a cofounder, which was the highest honor we could give him. He remains one of our favorite people and best friends. Unsurprisingly, he is the CEO of his own company now.

MOVING WITH THE MOMENTUM

When you sign a few deals and have some dollars coming in, you gain momentum, which is what we did at Buddy Media (thanks, Jeff!). So, it was time for us to start thinking about how we would support our clients. In the early days, Jeff was both selling and supporting with Abby's help. But with him and Mike—two powerhouse salespeople—pitching and closing deals so quickly, we needed someone to support the clients full time. Enter Mike Jaindl, or as we immediately called him, MJ.

MJ was another young gun who oozed promise. He graduated from Boston University in 2003 with a degree in information systems management and then worked for GE, where he learned and used the Six Sigma system to implement and streamline information technology solutions. We knew these were no-nonsense environments. MJ not only survived, but he thrived, winning one of the company's coveted GE Corporate Management Awards for "speed and quality of identity management implementation."

MJ came to Buddy Media as employee No. 5, and he was exactly what we needed—highly skilled, buttoned-up, smart, and kind—and quickly created the structure and processes that supported our clients after Jeff or Mike closed a deal.

We continued to grow and soon had close to ten employees cramped in an office on 60th and Broadway, and I knew we needed a more formalized human resources structure. Once you get to about ten employees, you need help on the overall people front, and that help comes from hiring someone with HR experience who will focus all or part of their time on all things people-related.

Leaders give lip service to the old adage that your people are your most valuable resources, but it's amazing how often entrepreneurs put off hiring someone for the HR role and responsibilities. They think they can get by without an expense that isn't directly related to creating revenue. However, they are wrong because revenues will suffer if they don't treat HR as a critical early investment.

Startups might be small in numbers, but they must move fast. If someone isn't proactively paying attention to the worries, confusion, and questions (and rumors) that employees share, it's easy (perhaps even inevitable) to miss the small cracks that develop. Unchecked cracks spread into large fissures within your company foundation. Employees need a safe, objective person they can turn to with their issues (and complaints), and the sooner you hire that person, the better.

At Buddy Media, I hired someone who could help me with HR functions like payroll and benefits, performance reviews, bonding events, building culture, and bookkeeping functions. This allowed me to keep my head above water, focus on finding, attracting, and hiring the right people, and building a cohesive team. Most importantly, it also signaled to our employees that I cared about them.

It wasn't until we pivoted to a SaaS company in late 2009 that our revenue really took off. Only then, with recurring revenue from happy customers, could we floor the gas and hire fast. And that's just what we did, and our employees helped us do it.

If you get it right with your first employees, you can rely on them to bring in their friends. Buddy Media employees were always our best brand evangelists and recruiters. If someone was successful in their job, odds were good they knew others like them who would be great hires.

We rewarded our employees (Buddies, as they named themselves) with a good chunk of money for every referral. At our all-team quarterly meetings I even showcased a leaderboard of the Buddies who had the most referrals to ensure everyone in the company knew how important hiring was and to add another incentive to the team. In the long run, this strategy saved us money and a great deal of time when it came to figuring out if a new hire would fit within our culture.

With a moneyball approach, we needed fewer utility players during the scaling phase and more specialists who filled singular roles. This was also when some employees earned promotions, some needed to move sideways or down in the organization, and new hires were brought in when necessary to supervise employees previously operating with great autonomy.

Moneyballing during this stage is particularly challenging because it involves changing the status quo, and some employees will resist new roles, responsibilities, and job titles. And if you make the mistake of adopting a "we don't get hung up on titles, so pick your own" attitude, many people will have inflated titles. Now you have the crappy task of resetting their expectations when you change their roles or bring in a more seasoned player above them. Frankly, you are better off having no titles than a team filled with inflated titles that will eventually pop like an overfilled balloon in a pin factory.

The scaling stage is also when you birth departments, so you must have a clear org chart and reporting structure with no overlap of roles and responsibilities. At Buddy Media, for example, we separated the customer success department from sales with MJ in charge. However, our hiring decisions were still driven by focusing on meeting our customers' needs and making sales easier as our products evolved and new features and functions were released.

DEALING WITH A CRAPPY HIRE

Even worse than hiring the wrong people is keeping those bad hires around.

No one hires the wrong person on purpose, just as no one takes a job thinking they will soon be fired. Everyone goes in with the best intentions, but everyone makes mistakes, and sometimes things just don't work out.

In theory, all founders know what to do when this happens: you should fire the employee. But operationalizing this truth is not easy. Entrepreneurs are typically eternal optimists (Mike) or chronic realists (Kass). And many are very stubborn and think they can always figure out how to make things work. As new entrepreneurs it's also tempting to give in to fear. The thought of telling people to pack up their personal belongings, turn in their keys, and hit the road can create paralysis.

This happened to us when Golf.com began to gain momentum. We hired our first salesperson, and let's just say he was no Jeff Ragovin. He was a really nice guy, but he didn't show up with two signed deals in his pocket. The only thing he successfully sold at Golf.com was himself.

Neither of us had ever fired anyone, but I (Mike) was in charge of sales and this employee reported to me. I asked Kass and Mike Caspar to leave our shared office, and I called in the employee to deliver the sad news. After about forty minutes, Caspar and Kass saw the soon-to-be-no-longer-employee walk out of the office in amazingly good spirits. He didn't appear bummed or sad. He looked pretty happy.

"How'd it go?" Kass and Caspar asked in unison when they returned to our office.

"Not too well," I said. "By the end, I told him he was doing a great job and gave him a promotion. And a raise. He made some *really* good arguments."

A few months later, we joined forces and told the salesperson it was time for him to leave. This didn't go well, but he didn't get another promotion and we no longer had an expense that produced no revenues. The lesson: firing people is HARD! But it has to be done, even if you, like Mike, are conflict-averse.

Not firing someone who isn't a good fit or can't meet their goals will only do the company and its employees a disservice. It costs the company money and time, as each hour lost dealing with issues created by the wrong hires is another hour spent not building a better product, selling it, or supporting it. These are dollars and hours you can't afford to lose and will never get back. Plus, keeping employees around when they aren't a good fit often leads to resentment among the rest of the team.

One of the founder's most important jobs is to ensure the team has everything it needs to succeed. If they have what they need but aren't performing, act fast. Get them on a performance improvement plan (PIP) as soon as possible, and then get them out if they still can't step up.

A PIP is a formal written document that outlines the areas of performance that an employee is falling short on, as well as the specific steps an employee must take over a certain period of time to improve and meet the expectations of their job. There's no set template for a PIP, but it should be in writing and delivered in person with the goal of being crystal clear on what is needed of the employee.

This is particularly hard when someone has been with the company for a few years or more. The unfortunate reality for startups is that not everyone scales. When you hit growth stages, you often have to make tough choices about whether certain individuals can withstand the speed and demands that are about to be put on them.

No one is immune to this scrutiny—even founders, who also don't always scale. Some are more suited for running a profitable, low-growth small business and are perfectly fine with that. Others are great starters and maybe good builders, but they aren't scalers or sustainers. If they lack self-awareness, are slaves to their huge egos, and insist on being the stars of the show—and let's face it, this is pretty common among entrepreneurs—then they aren't likely to move on to their next big idea. Instead, they are destined to play an unwanted role in the company: destroyer.

In 2011, we faced several key moneyball decisions while scaling Buddy Media. We were now focused on taking the company public through a listing on either NASDAQ or the New York Stock Exchange. To go public, we knew we needed to build a world-class sales and support organization. Our team was scrappy and awesome. But we were the first to admit that we had never scaled a company into hundreds of millions in revenue, which was our goal.

While we already had plans to promote Jeff to cofounder, the three of us realized we also needed someone to help us recruit a global sales team to ensure we hit our aggressive sales numbers each quarter, a requisite for being a public company.

We had started the recruiting process, and our eyes were set on Susan St. Ledger, a long-time Salesforce executive who had brought in many of Salesforce's largest customers. To boot, she was a superstar in Marc Benioff's eyes, and I (Kass) knew it would be a huge win for us if we could persuade her to jump Salesforce's ship.

Mike and I both flew to the Bay Area to take her to one of her favorite restaurants, The Village Pub in Woodside. After a tense negotiation that had us going back and forth to San Francisco three times over a few months, followed by an aggressive attempt by Marc to retain her, Susan joined us as president of Buddy Media.

Susan brought huge credibility to our company and our mission of going public. And although Mike technically managed Susan, I would argue that Susan pretty much managed Mike! Most of Susan's meetings with Mike and Jeff went something like this.

Susan: "Why are you doing it like this?"

Mike and Jeff: "We don't know any other way."

Susan: "This makes no sense. We need to do it like this."

Mike: "OK. Then let's do it like that."

It is safe to say we would never have positioned the company to go public without Susan. She was a real pro with the playbook we needed and was worth every cent we paid her (in cash and stock, which turned out to be a nice payday for her!)

Informing Susan months later that she was returning to Salesforce after it agreed to purchase Buddy Media was one of the most terrifying conversations we had ever had with an employee. Luckily, the deal meant millions for her, so she took it quite well and has done much bigger and better things, such as building the sales armies for publicly listed companies Okta, Splunk, and HashiCorp.

LOOKING FOR FIT

When you define a role your company needs, the job description tells you the skills you want that person to bring and how many years of experience you want the person to have. That's typically the easy part. If you need someone to sell your product, you hire someone who knows how to sell stuff (and has a proven track record!). If you need someone who can drive a forklift, you hire someone who is certified to drive a forklift and has been doing so for many years.

However, our hiring successes and failures have told us that other essentials aren't as obvious.

For instance, I (Kass) look for clues about a candidate's emotional intelligence (EQ). Do they know what they know and, more importantly, what they don't know?

And I (Mike) look for clues that tell me new hires aren't procrastinators or blame shifters—they attack their work, take accountability for getting it done, and are team-focused players who encourage the people around them.

We prioritize hiring people who share our company's values. At Buddy Media, some values we prioritized were hard work, transparency, honesty, doing the right thing, giving back, believing that you don't know everything, and raising others up.

These things boil down to cultural fit, and as the next chapter will demonstrate, you will never put the right cult in your culture without hiring people who fit.

CUTTING THROUGH THE CRAP: KEY LESSONS LEARNED

- Follow your financials and big-rock priorities to ensure you hire for the right positions once you start the company.
- Initially, you will need to hire more utility players—employees who will wear multiple hats.
- You must always moneyball—not only hire the right people at whatever stage you're in, but also field them in their optimal position.
- Moneyballing changes over time as your company grows—not everyone scales. Be prepared. Firing those who don't fit is a necessary part of the process.
- Incentivize current employees to recruit other great employees. Rarely will great employees introduce weak prospects to the company.
- Have difficult conversations sooner rather than later. The longer you wait to cut an underperformer loose, the more cracks will develop in your company's foundation.

PUTTING THE CULT IN YOUR CULTURE

THE SHOVELING THAT COMES WITH CREATING A CRAP-FREE CULTURE.

Melissa Bromberg and I (Kass) were lab partners for ninth-grade biology when our teacher, Mrs. Lamphere, introduced us to petri dishes. Frankly, I was not that jazzed. All of that microscopic crap growing grossed me out.

My childhood and early adulthood, however, served as a petri dish for how to (and how not to) grow another type of culture that fascinates me—team cultures.

Growing up the youngest of four siblings in a dysfunctional family wasn't fun. But it profoundly impacted my determination to create the culture at my companies that I never experienced as a child.

This meant building a culture in which we took the work seriously but not ourselves. It meant developing a supportive, warm family atmosphere where everyone felt respected, appreciated, and valued. And it meant creating meaningful work so that team members believed they were part of something bigger than themselves. I wanted to bring together a tight-knit group of

A-players who worked hard, laughed, cared about each other, celebrated life together, and, if we were lucky, made a little money along the way!

Thankfully, Mike shared that vision, and we have made culture a high priority in every company we have led. We did not always achieve this nirvana. But nothing was more vital to Buddy Media's success than our culture.

USING RITUAL TO TURN YOUR CULTURE INTO A CULT

Most founders and executives spend considerable time, as we have always done, focusing on how to best manage their companies. This is important. But managing your business and creating your culture are different, although joined at the hip. Many well-run companies have a lousy culture. They can thrive, but at what cost to the organization?

Magic happens only when great culture meets world-class management.

For instance, take the dreaded employee handbook. We had one for each company and recommend you have one as well. Employment law is too thorny to try to fly blind. The handbook outlines the company's rules and policies, hours of operation, and holidays, and covers employment discrimination and harassment policies, paid sick leaves, the Family Medical Leave Act, and data access policies. These are the company's laws. Break them, and you may be fired for cause.

What the handbook does not include is the sum of the behaviors and ethics, beliefs, values, traditions, and symbols that constitute a company's culture.

A company's culture is like air—nowhere and everywhere simultaneously. It is invisible and ubiquitous. You can feel it even if you can't see it, and so can your employees and customers.

The handbook makes it clear that employees cannot harass each other. A good culture repeatedly reinforces the norms—mutual respect, empathy, and accountability, for instance—that make harassment undesirable and unacceptable among employees. Good culture encourages team members to pick each other up rather than push them down, give each other the benefit of the doubt, and assume the best intentions rather than demonizing one another and assuming the worst.

A radically good company culture is the closest we get at work to the love we share with people outside the office. It is the glue every team needs to hold it together—industrial-strength, multi-purpose, people-bonding superglue.

So before you even make your first hire, you need to start cultivating the cult you want in that culture.

The cult?

The word *cult* often connotes the worst of humanity—a group that manipulates members to the benefit of a charismatic leader. This, however, is the modern evolution of the term. The Latin word *cultus*, from which it is derived, conveys a sense of adoration and has given us the words *culture* and *cultivation*, which do not carry such negativity.

You can't spell *culture* without *cult*. It is your job as the founder to clarify what your cult stands for. And there is no better way to develop a cult of positivity and understanding than with rituals and beliefs—the set of consistent values, actions, and traditions—that drive the behaviors you want to instill in your company's ethos.

So, what are some of these beliefs and rituals we have used to make company culture our superglue?

MAKE YOUR VISION, VALUES, AND ORIGIN STORY TANGIBLE

Humans love stories. Always have. Always will. They are fundamental to the human experience and not found among other animals, even the most intelligent.

Your origin story, which you will tell repeatedly, includes why you were driven to create your company. It is pregnant with your vision for the world you are trying to create and the values you hold most dear.

Craft your origin story carefully. You are in a unique position to write the script. Don't blow it by ignoring it. Write it down clearly and succinctly, and share it widely. All great organizations, from religious movements to global companies, have their script. Make yours relevant and compelling.

Steve Jobs and Steve Wozniak had a vision to create an easy-to-use computer and bestowed the vision with principles that have guided the company ever since. Marc Benioff has repeatedly told how his time at Oracle selling expensive on-premise software set him on a journey to create an "internet company/site for Sales Force Automation." In his very first one-page planning document, he included values like "world-class organization," speed, and "usability (Amazon quality)," and he captured the story with his own symbol of hope, the ubiquitous no-software mark.[*]

---

[*] Benioff, Marc, and Carlye Adler. *Behind the Cloud: The Untold Story of How Salesforce.com Went from Idea to Billion-Dollar Company-and Revolutionized an Industry.* Jossey-Bass, 2009.

So, shout your story from the top of your mountain—to investors, the media, friends on social media, vendors, and everyone you hire.

Buddy Media set out to help companies market in an entirely new way. Consumers were spending more and more time on social media sites, and companies needed to adapt. Our shared values of transparency, accountability, hard work, customer centricity, and fun were also important to our story. We ensured employees not only heard and knew them but lived and breathed them.

RECRUIT AND ONBOARD NEW MEMBERS PURPOSEFULLY (KASS)

When we interviewed potential employees, I did my best to manage their expectations before they ever accepted an offer to work with us.

"Come work with us," I would say. "I can't promise that you will always love what you do, but I promise you will like working here more than you don't. You're going to be surrounded by very smart people, and you are going to laugh. If Mike and I do our jobs right, your slice of this company will be worth something, a nest egg, a chunk of change for your future."

We backed up these words with consistent actions that began *during* the recruiting process. Early interactions with candidates are as important as winning the heart and mind of a potential mate on your first few dates. Make each interaction count.

At Buddy Media, our recruiting team (led by the amazing Pam Schloss) created a process that went above and beyond. She and her team did their best to deduce whether someone fit our culture well before the start date. For an early-stage company, cultural fit is more important than skill set. Employees who don't share your values and missions can infect the culture you are building. We wanted team-focused players who lifted people up rather than wearing them down.

When a candidate said yes to an offer, Pam and her team sent a gift as a token that we appreciated them and saw them as a person with passions and hobbies outside of work. These welcome gifts were often personalized based on the interests they shared during the interview exploration process.

Some companies ignore employees on their first day yet underwrite "goodbye lunches" for departing employees. This makes no sense. Celebrate every hire on the way in! Starting a new job is always nerve-wracking no matter how experienced you are. A positive onboarding experience is critical to how someone feels about their initial time at a company.

PROTECT YOUR CULT

In addition to setting up and supporting the right type of cult, there's the ongoing need for vigilance to protect what you are creating.

Buddy Media, for instance, had grown to about twenty-five people when I noticed some "clique-ish" behaviors among a few veterans who weren't welcoming new hires in the open and friendly way we expected. I quickly called a meeting with the relevant players and shared specific examples of what I saw happening that were counter to our culture. I boiled it down and didn't mince words.

"We welcome new people into this company period, pencil down. Unsupportive actions will not happen here. If they do, you will be fired," I said. And I was serious.

Managing a team isn't just about job performance. Cultural performance also matters. To protect the values of your culture, a leader has to spot the places where those values are under attack and, as my dad always told me, be quick and decisive to counterattack.

CREATE TEAM GAMES TO BUILD CAMARADERIE

As a new Buddy, you were born into either the Green Team or Blue Team and would be a member of that team for the duration of your employment. (I might have gotten this idea from the "sorting hat" and "house cup championship" in the Harry Potter novels. But I digress . . .)

Some of our all-team meetings included games anyone could participate in and enjoy, regardless of athleticism. A favorite was our annual spring kickball game. Most people can kick a big red ball. Even if it only went a few feet (like mine), it didn't matter because the laughing and cheering brought us together.

Another effective activity was our scavenger hunt. Teams of four (all from different departments and a mix between those on the Blue and Green teams) raced into different boroughs of New York City to complete tasks. My favorites were taking a picture of the team sitting on a New York Fire Department fire truck and delivering cupcakes to my cousin Julia's office.

We compiled the photos after these events, projected them at the dinners afterward, and hung them across the office as reminders of our mutual joy and respect.

These teams created a sense of belonging throughout Buddy Media. Buddies identified with and took pride in their teams. They kept their team-colored headbands on their desk and wore their team T-shirts to work even when there was no activity. They got to know coworkers they might never have known because they shared a team spirit and bond. And we knew that regardless of which team won, the bonding among and between the members was immense.

INSTILL GIVING INTO THE REGULAR COURSE OF BUSINESS

There is no better way to create culture than to ensure the company stands for something bigger than its products and services. The most potent way we found to do this is by applying the diverse skill sets we assembled to benefit others outside the company.

Doing well (i.e., making money) and doing good (i.e., helping others) aren't mutually exclusive. From making a thousand sandwiches for a shelter during the annual scavenger hunt to buying and donating toys during our annual holiday event, we incorporated giving back as a core value.

Our tentpole program was Cycle for Survival, a fundraiser started in 2007 by our good friends Dave and Jen Linn at the Equinox cycling studio across from our first office near Columbus Circle. I (Mike) went to Northwestern with Dave, and we loved Jen from the first day we met her. We were quick to get behind the event. It's hard to say no to a friend after she is diagnosed with a rare form of cancer. And it was impossible to say no to Jen, healthy or not.

We got involved because we wanted to help. Employees started to notice our promotion of the event and fundraising efforts, and several of them joined the effort. Within two years, we had more than a hundred Buddies participating—not because we mandated it, but because we offered an opportunity to do good together.[*]

---

[*] You and your company can participate, too! Learn more at cycleforsurvival.org.

Jen visited our office in March 2011. She spoke about how "inspiring and motivating" it was to see Buddy Media raising money to fund therapies to treat her rare cancer as Cycle for Survival's first corporate team.

Fast-forward to 2024, and 66 percent of the $33 million raised to fund cancer research came from corporate teams. Some of these are led by former Buddy Media team members who have started their own companies and have successfully made giving and Cycle for Survival a part of their culture-building efforts.

Jen, Buddy Media's champion, would have been so proud of the growth of Cycle for Survival's corporate initiatives. Unfortunately for the world, she died four months after her final talk at the Buddy Media offices. The twelve rounds of chemotherapy, six surgeries, and more pain than any of us could even imagine finally took her from us. We are confident that Buddy Media's success with the fundraiser would have been a fraction of the size without her inspiration, and we know that she is with every Buddy to this day.

To honor Jen, we wanted to expand our giving program and make it the centerpiece of Buddy Media's business philosophy. The goal was to shift from giving on weekends and evenings to giving as part of the flow of everyday life. With help from Jen and philanthropy experts, we crafted a plan to create Give4, an ambitious program that would donate 2 percent of Buddy Media's revenue and 2 percent of the team's time to a new foundation dedicated to solving the world's most pressing issues. We also planned to recruit other innovative companies to do the same.

In August 2011, shortly after Jen's death, we presented it to our board. Our argument was simple: "Giving isn't a byproduct of great businesses," we wrote in bold letters on the presentation. "It causes great businesses to be built."

We still believe this to our core, and we were bummed that the board rejected the idea. It's no coincidence that part of what attracted us to sell to Salesforce versus the other interested buyers was how Marc Benioff fully integrated philanthropy and the Salesforce Foundation into all the company did. Marc's innovative 1:1:1 program—1 percent of time, 1 percent of profits, and 1 percent of equity—was created at the very beginning of Salesforce.

We are convinced that Jen played a role in our sale to Salesforce. We'd like to think Marc would have loved and been equally inspired by fearless Jen. So, find your Jen and let her infuse giving into your culture, just like Jen did for us.

To honor Jen, 10 percent of gross sales from this book will be donated to Cycle for Survival.*

BUY BALLOONS AND CUPCAKES (KASS)

I have a very simple theory about balloons: balloons make people happy. Have you ever had a balloon when you didn't feel something good was happening? Even in hospitals, balloons are given to signal recovery is underway!

When the company turned four, I, along with our head of operations and the HR and recruiting teams, blew up thousands of balloons and placed them across our 3,500-square-foot office on the morning of the anniversary. When employees walked out of the elevator, balloons collapsed around them while the HR team greeted them with mimosas and breakfast pastries. This was our

---

* To learn more, visit www.shovelingshit.com.

way of saying "congrats and thank you." Everyone shared the experience of parting the foot-deep sea of green and blue balloons as they made their way from the elevator to their desks!

We are big believers that celebrations create a strong glue in a culture. I proactively looked for opportunities to make them happen. We celebrated birthdays with cupcakes for everyone, and cards signed by Mike and me were sent to the employees' homes, usually with a gift card included.

In fact, balloons and cupcakes became synonymous with celebrations at Buddy Media, and we highly recommend them as you plan ways to celebrate your milestones.

RECOGNIZE EMPLOYEES EARLY, OFTEN, AND PUBLICLY

The vast majority of employees today don't feel appreciated.[*] This takes a major toll on productivity as employees who feel appreciated are more engaged. Creating a culture of recognition and appreciation is easy and inexpensive if you proactively develop programs to show productive employees the love.

Many of the recognitions we provided were specific and based on individuals and teams surpassing goals. Others were to thank teams (like accounting) that often flew under the radar but played a vital role in our operational success. When we closed a big deal or released a new product, we celebrated as an entire company,

---

[*] "Two-Thirds (67%) of Employed Americans Feel Appreciation at Work is in Short Supply According to New Blueboard Report." *PR Newswire,* February 16, 2023. https://www.prnewswire.com/news-releases/two-thirds-67-of-employed-americans-feel-appreciation-at-work-is-in-short-supply-according-to-new-blueboard-report-301748164.html.

usually with food and company-wide recognition of the team members who drove the success.

Celebrations were not just for company milestones but individual ones as well. This helped our hard-working team members feel appreciated. For a one-year anniversary, for instance, Buddies received a custom bobblehead made in their likeness. I would surprise the employee with the look-alike, so they never knew when I would do it.

The first anniversary of a team member's hire was a big deal to me. I was often called the Executor. I would execute all of our plans, and I was super intentional about "executing" employees within 45-60 days if they weren't working out. If you made it past that, the team knew you would be a contributor who pulled your weight. And the custom, personalized bobbleheads, which cost a pretty penny, symbolized the value of great employees.

On second anniversaries, employees received the coveted "I'm a Deal-Maker" mug that tied back to the onboarding process in which I encouraged them to have "a deal-maker, not a deal-breaker" mindset. This was more than just another coffee cup; it took on cult symbol status!

The third anniversary was commemorated with a 20-inch-tall trophy that said, "I'm a Somebuddy." It was a Buddy Media monument to longevity.

On fourth anniversaries, Buddies were given a branded piece of luggage and a large bronzed trophy of a globe that said, "You're A Worldclass Buddy." We sold the company before we could do fifth anniversary awards. We were happy to learn that Salesforce had its own system to recognize employees.

These were just a few of the regular ways we showed our appreciation, and all were public in nature. Objects were displayed proudly on desks (which is why we could never decrease the size of desks!) and became symbols of employees leveling up in the organization. Mike's bobblehead and Somebuddy trophy is proudly displayed today in his office. (His deal-maker mug is in our kitchen cabinet.)

COMMIT TO A COMPANY CALENDAR

Organizations that endure have traditions. Doing something on a regular schedule makes rituals important and non-negotiable. They become just the way things are done. Traditions matter in establishing and maintaining a positive cult.

Buddy Media's quarterly all-team meetings and the team events that followed—where we celebrated together—became important glue. No one even questioned whether they would attend unless a personal or family emergency arose.

These were not easy to pull off and involved a ton of shoveling. Work we had to pull off for each quarterly event included creating a lengthy presentation from the two of us and our management team, organizing a giving activity like the ones we've already mentioned, planning a fun group activity and arranging an all-team dinner event afterward. We shoveled hard to make each event awesome, and by over-investing in these, they took on mythic status.

Some might wonder if all the planning and hard work required to pull this off are worth the effort. And some may question the frequency or costs. We would ask, "What is the return on investment from a team that is empowered, fired up, and connected to each other deeply?" These days helped instill our culture into the company and were important both during our startup phase and as we started to scale and add dozens of employees a quarter.

The day-long gatherings were scheduled a year in advance and often went well into the night. They were purposefully crafted to reinforce our values.

To kick off each meeting, we presented to employees as if they were the board and we worked for them—*here are our revenues, here are our expenses, here's where we're spending money, here's how much we have in the bank.*

Many other founders thought we were crazy for sharing full financial results. At the time, we were one of the hottest companies in New York City and the subject of considerable media coverage. So, many thought the risk that the information would leak to the press far outweighed the benefits. But not once did a Buddy leak the information. Employees felt trusted and empowered with the information we shared.

We also brought in speakers (usually board members, investors, or clients) so everyone could learn something about the company simultaneously. Many, like Jen, were meant to inspire.

The Halloween all-team meeting provided an opportunity for another favorite tradition. Everyone had to come to work in costume, and we gave out monetary prizes for the best individual and group costumes (online voting, of course).

When I (Kass) first told the management team that dressing up was non-negotiable, I got pushback from our newly appointed chief technology officer, Patrick Stokes. Let's just say Patrick wasn't a fan of wearing a costume. But I told him, "We are going to lead by example. Everyone dresses up." He relented and made a huge effort by wearing a long, neon green (tight!) onesie the entire day—even outside as we walked to a group lunch (which we all remember and some of us can't not remember).

During the holidays, we carried on a team bonding tradition I learned from my days at Jaffe Associates. After the all-team meeting in December, I gave every employee $100 to buy a gift for another employee. Names were drawn from a hat, and you couldn't get someone on your team. You had two hours to find and buy the gift, and then we met at a lunch spot where the gifts were given out.

It wasn't just about giving the gift, however. They also had to explain *why* they chose the gift. This experience created communication across departments because Buddies asked other Buddies for information about the person they were buying a gift for.

As this tradition continued, I loved that employees would start dropping hints. The closer we got to the event, the more often I could hear people say things like, "I do need a new hat. I'm just saying in case anyone needs to know." Or, "I lost my gloves on the train the other day." Nothing made me happier.

We started this tradition when we had just ten employees and continued it even after we had more than 250, because we valued the bonding experience and the generosity and thoughtfulness displayed by the gift-givers every year.

THE HALLMARKS OF A GOOD CULT CULTURE

We used these rituals, traditions, and much more to create Buddy Media's cult-like status as a great workplace. You need to create ones that work for you and your company. You will know when they work as you will see and feel it daily. Are people smiling? Do you hear belly laughs every now and then? Are they showing up to work (not just on time, but are they *showing up*)? Do they have a sense of purpose?

You will also see it in your metrics to gauge employee health—your employee engagement surveys and retention rates. Our retention rate for employees who were at Buddy Media for at least one year was more than 95 percent. We measured this closely as this metric is a great sign of loyalty and culture. If great employees walk out the door, there's a reason. And it's probably you, not them.

You will see it in the way employees recruit new employees. Even with financial incentives no one will stick a friend in an awful job just to earn a few bucks. If your culture is solid, however, they will eagerly recruit new players because they want their most talented friends to experience what they are experiencing, personally and professionally. During one year at Buddy Media, more than half of our new hires were referred by current employees.

You also will see it in the way employees connect even after they no longer work together.

We were working on this very chapter when we got a text from Wes Barrow, a Buddy who is now a tech investor in New York City.

"Hello," he texted in April of 2024. "Could we have a Buddy Media reunion soon? Hope y'all are well."

This text came nearly twelve years after we sold Buddy Media to Salesforce!

Our last major Buddy Media reunion, also requested by and organized by Buddies, was in 2017, five years after Salesforce purchased the business. We supported it by hosting it at our favorite place, Hill Country Barbecue Market in New York, a space full of Buddy Media nostalgia. This is where we got together after many of our all-team meetings.

Let's invite former employees to join us and just hang out, former Buddies emailed us. *Who knows if anyone will show up, but we will have a good time either way.*

More than one hundred Buddies showed up, and we handed out T-shirts that said "#buddies4life." Clearly, the culture outlived their employment with Buddy Media!

Another way you'll know you have a positive cult—and perhaps the most important way—is that you will see it when the crap hits the fan. If you are running out of money and employees agree to stay on board without pay, you are on to something. You want a resilient company, and that comes from a culture in which people care about their work and about each other enough to push through adversity.

Rest assured, you and your employees will go through bad times, uncertain times, pivots, changes, and losses. You don't want people jumping ship because they feel lost, uncertain about their work, or worse, uncertain of you as the founder(s). When things start slipping off the rails, for individuals or your business, you will know you have a quality cult in your culture by the way everyone rallies to get back on track together.

Culture will be a critical part of your success. And like everything else, it doesn't just happen on your own. You need to work hard shoveling to make it happen. Manage your company with excellence, and you will be well on your way to closing the gap between your vision and reality.

CUTTING THROUGH THE CRAP: KEY LESSONS LEARNED

- Over-communicate the values of the organization.
- To be successful, cultivate a positive cult every day and in everything you do—during recruiting, team events, communication, etc.

- When hiring, cultural fit is more important than skill set fit, and your employees will often become your best recruiters.
- Protect your cult at all costs.
- Make giving an everyday part of the culture.
- Create regular, meaningful activities (games are good) that connect you to employees and employees to each other.
- Celebrate together.
- Acknowledge each other often.

LEADERS SHOVEL FIRST

THE CRAP THAT COMES WITH LEADING A STARTUP.

When I (Kass) landed a job with law firm marketing agency Jaffe & Associates in 1995, one of the greatest perks was working near my father.

Jaffe's offices were in the same building as my dad's firm, Howrey & Simon, which he led as managing partner from 1985 to 2000.

At six feet, three inches, my dad was a born leader—the former captain of the Iona University basketball team, the one-time vice-chairman and assistant dean of Temple Law School, and then the head honcho at one of the world's largest and most respected litigation firms. Dad managed more than one thousand employees in eighteen offices around the globe. Working at Jaffe allowed me to witness his leadership in one of the most high-stakes environments imaginable.

One day, Ashley Seeger, a friend and coworker, and I walked by the fishbowl conference room where my dad was leading what seemed like a solemn meeting with his top lieutenants. He rose from his chair, his suit jacket off, revealing his 1990s suspenders with the scales of justice on them. He enthusiastically waved to us, and stepped out of the meeting to greet us with high-fives and a big smile.

"How are you two doing?!" he asked.

It was as if nothing was more important to him than us, even though he was in the middle of a business conversation. This small gesture let us know we mattered.

This was common for my father at work. He gave people the license to be human at a time when humanity had been all but stripped from business. His leadership resulted in both a positive culture and a profitable business.

Whether leading a team or coaching me in basketball or tennis, he consistently provided constructive criticism and positive reinforcement, communicated shared values (tenacity was his favorite!), demanded accountability, and led with humor. I got my love of competition and laughter from him, two qualities that have served me well in every area of life, including as an entrepreneur.

In addition to emulating the *way* he led, I also learned the importance of prioritizing the art of leadership as a driver of operational success. The commitment to operating a world-class organization at every stage of its development doesn't happen without intentional effort from the top. Leaders set the tone and create priorities; their management styles often cascade through an organization. You must get this right from the beginning and continue to evolve as you scale.

More ink has been spilled on leadership advice than any other business topic. Our take on it is based on what we've gleaned from other leaders (like my father) and the many hard lessons we learned while shoveling with our teams over the years.

USE COMPENSATION TO ALIGN INTERESTS

The battle for top talent is intense. While financial compensation is not the only tool in a leader's toolkit, it is important for shaping results. Nothing aligns human activity more than fully aligned financial incentives.

Paying a living wage and competitive salaries are table stakes. For your compensation to influence culture and productivity, your total financial benefits must convey that you value people and don't just see them as cogs in a money-making machine.

We love rewarding team members with spot bonuses. Small amounts of cash show our appreciation and are felt immediately, unlike raises paid over twenty-four pay periods per year. In the early stages, when money is particularly tight for most startups, this isn't always practical. But if you land a new account, for instance, and can spread a little love without breaking the bank, it is well worth the investment.

Your compensation program should focus on aligning the company's interests with the interests of employees because this creates an environment of accountability. Use raises and bonuses strategically as incentives for the behaviors you want to see. Tie both to performance. Promote team members based on their contributions. This creates a meritocracy where those performing move up, setting an example for what it takes to advance.

Effective reviews are an important part of the process, and leaders influence them not only by participating but by establishing the company's policies and approach to giving feedback. Effective reviews should include specific examples of what an employee has done well or poorly and clear expectations and measurable goals for the coming year.

Consistent feedback throughout the year, followed by annual reviews, allows you to tie performance to compensation and ensure everyone knows what drives decisions. And this isn't something you can put off until you've established the business. We began the review process the first year we started each business because it's just as important when you have six employees as when you have six hundred.

We also love ownership for employees.

The most recent data shows that in 2021, there were more than 6,500 employee stock ownership plans (ESOPs) in the US, with more than 14.7 million participants. Around five thousand plans technically didn't qualify as ESOPs but provided employees with some form of profit sharing.* That wasn't the standard when we started Golf.com or Buddy Media, but 100 percent of our employees had some stock (after a vesting period, of course).

This was an operational leadership decision that had a powerful influence on the culture of our companies. Sharing the pie gives employees a sense of ownership (as well as actual ownership). It transforms the team mindset so employees take responsibility and not lunch breaks when the pressure is on and the work is challenging. They are all-in rather than worried about how soon they can clock out. And it creates an incentive for sticking with the company.

---

* "Employee Ownership by the Numbers." *National Center for Employee Ownership,* February 2024. https://www.nceo.org/articles/employee-ownership-by-the-numbers.

In 2007, our board questioned giving stock to every employee regardless of their level and experience. However, we were convinced that the benefits of having teams that thought and acted more as owners than employees far outweighed the dilution we took from giving up part of the company.

The best types of compensation, however, often come in non-monetary forms. In addition to competitive vacation packages and the standard days off for holidays, for instance, we closed the office on the Thursday and Friday of Thanksgiving and the entire week between Christmas and New Year's, and we encouraged a no-email-on-vacation policy that applied to everyone but the founders and our senior-most leaders.

We offered other perks to show our appreciation, like giving every employee credit toward buying sneakers once a year, intended to encourage exercise. We also had our "Lost Lunches"—a free lunch for anyone who wanted to join us to watch and analyze an episode of the (incredibly frustrating) television show *Lost*.

When creating these types of perks it's essential to consider how they will scale with the company. If employees expect new shoes once a year, what happens when you grow from a dozen employees to five hundred?

PROMOTE FROM WITHIN WHENEVER POSSIBLE

One of the more considerable leadership challenges for entrepreneurs is managing the career opportunities that come with a growing company.

The best leaders cultivate environments that prioritize employees' professional growth. Employees want to know you have a path for them to grow. The easiest way to achieve this is to promote from within when possible. I (Kass) often repeated a mantra that established expectations about moving up in the company: "Do the job you have and the one you want." This helped squash potential complaints and increase focus. I also think that by regularly verbalizing it, employees knew I saw their hard work and that they would be promoted when the time was right.

Not everyone, of course, has what it takes to manage people effectively. While management skills can be taught, the best managers are born with the innate leadership characteristics others lack—empathy, emotional intelligence, integrity, communication skills, and humility. So be careful when promoting employees to managerial roles. Do so only when you see someone doing their job *and* leading from within their team.

CLARIFY THE ROLES

Everyone must do their part for your startup's story to play out how you envision. That starts with everyone knowing their part. A team wins (and loses) together, and most employees want to know how their work fits into the story. It's the leader's responsibility to tell them.

Not only do employees need to know their roles, but yours as well. The founders are viewed as the ship's captains, and sometimes, the crew will wonder what the captains do that keeps the boat afloat. So, everyone needs to know how the company is organized and the roles the leaders play.

We made it clear that Mike was raising money to fund the company and overseeing the sales team and that I was the go-to person for HR, marketing, and other operations. We then explained what each person in our management team did to avoid confusion about roles and responsibilities within the company. This clarity was missing at Shape Matrix and contributed to the difficulty we had commercializing the technology.

In the early days, an org chart might not be needed (we always provided one). As you grow, it's essential to reduce confusion and enhance communication.

BE THE BOSS, NOT THE BUDDY

Your role isn't to be best friends with everyone, so clarifying your part in the story includes establishing clear boundaries. You can care for your employees (in fact, that's essential) and have some level of friendship, but you and they need to know there are limits to the personal relationship.

This is a significant challenge for leaders of any organization, not just entrepreneurs, because it's easy for the lines to blur when you work hard with people you appreciate, enjoy being around, and who share your same work ethic and values.

We had very close relationships with our management team, and I (Kass) considered Brittany White—my "Number 2"—a close personal friend. But startups suffer when founders cannot make decisions with a clear head involving their "friends," like promoting them when they don't deserve it, failing to fire them when they should be gone, ignoring unauthorized spending, or disregarding unprofessional behaviors.

We've worked with several founders who found themselves on this slippery slope. Some had allowed their top employees to spend without accountability and expense whatever they wanted back to the company. Others were awarded promotions and raises based more on personal relationships than merit. As a result, we had to help these founders make the painful moves that ended the uncontrolled spending or moved people into their appropriate roles, which, in some cases, was the unemployment line.

DON'T SHINE THE TURD

A new page turns every day in a company's story. Everyone doesn't always have access to the latest twists and turns in the plot. Leaders who want the whole team to move toward the company's mission, however, must communicate transparently and regularly about the financial health of the business and the wins as well as the losses.

This is a leadership lesson we learned from an investor at Golf.com. One day, I (Mike) was putting an overly positive spin on some less-than-stellar sales results, and Matt Sirovich, a board member, interrupted me and bluntly said, "I'm only going to say this once. Don't shine the turd. You tell us the good, the bad, and the ugly every time you get on this call."

The takeaway was simple: Matt was OK with bad news. He wasn't OK with surprises, with burying the bad news, or with "shining" the news to make a turd look like a pretty rock. We quickly adopted the concept, and the phrase became a mantra in our leadership communications philosophy.

When the results suck, great leaders do three things. They take ownership immediately. They share the news transparently. And they communicate a plan that addresses the underlying causes. If you step in manure, everyone will smell it. There's no point in acting as if it's not on your shoes. Own it quickly. Clean it up. And move on.

By practicing this as leaders, we created a culture where employees felt like trusted partners because they were empowered with information. They spoke up about issues and shared much more of the not-so-good news than they would have had we not set the example.

BE MINDFUL OF MEETINGS

Meetings can encourage creativity, troubleshoot issues, and drive efficiency in your teams. Or they can suck the life out of your organization. So, the challenge for leaders isn't to eliminate meetings but eliminate bad meetings and become efficient with the ones you have.

There's no cookie-cutter formula, but how you lead your meetings will become an example others will use to lead theirs.

First, you need a purpose for every meeting. Always write an agenda that begins with a clear understanding of what you want to achieve. Are you sharing information (explanation)? Seeking information and ideas (engagement)? Making a decision? Assessing a project (feedback)? Knowing what you need to achieve with a meeting is the best way to keep it from veering off track or being a total waste of time.

Second, be intentional about who is included in meetings, how long they last, how frequently they occur, and how people interact. All those things might change depending on the purpose of the meeting, but one thing should always be consistent: frank, transparent communication from the leader.

At Buddy Media, our top-priority meeting was the weekly gathering of our management team. We kept these as small as possible. One leader represented each department or area of the company, and attendance was mandatory. Founders often invite more people, or the wrong people, to their weekly leadership meetings. Then, when scaling, some people must be uninvited as more skilled managers take their place. Keep it tight from the beginning; include only the highest-level leaders and empower them to communicate what is necessary to their teams.

In addition to sharing information that was pushed out to all the teams in the company, we used our leadership team meetings to discuss and agree on significant changes.

For instance, this was the only time we changed our product roadmap. Too often founders allow changes to their roadmaps at any time without complete agreement and communication with their leadership team. This almost always backfires. Issues are usually missed by not intentionally discussing the implications of changes across all departments, and the leaders who were not a part of the decision can become resentful. Only make changes to your roadmap when everyone is together. Some may not like the decision, but everyone will agree about why it was made and the potential ramifications.

Finally, conflicts and passive aggressiveness among our leadership team or other teams within the company were teased out during these meetings. It was the time to discuss everything for the company's betterment so the team could move forward effectively as one.

DO THE DIRTY WORK

There's an old adage that you shouldn't ask an employee to do something you wouldn't do. That's crap. Often, you hire employees precisely because they can do things you *wouldn't do* simply because you *can't do* them. However, a willingness to humbly do the things you *can do* to help shovel crap at every level of the company is a powerful trust-builder and sets an example for others to follow.

You are no better than anyone else, so step up, help put up the holiday lights, stuff the marketing mailers, and clean up after the office party. Encourage the other leaders on your team to do the same and lead by example.

EMPOWER, DON'T MICROMANAGE

Entrepreneurs invest their hearts and souls into a startup, not to mention their time and money. With everything riding on the business's success, it's only natural to want to ensure everything is done to your satisfaction. This, however, can lead to counterproductive micromanagement that can destroy a culture and slow things down considerably.

As I (Kass) learned from my mentor and longtime friend Jeff Berman, one key to building and leading teams is to develop what he calls an "empowerment culture."

Jeff was one of my close friends in high school and college, and we reconnected in 2009 around our business interests when he was president of sales and marketing at MySpace.com. He then joined Buddy Media's board in 2010 and was someone I could lean on, complain to, and ask for help. Jeff stressed that an empowerment culture requires more than merely delegating assignments like a dealer tossing out cards in a casino. It means working together to set goals and assess the resources needed.

"Once you empower your team," Jeff told me, "your job is to get out of everyone's way. Their job is to be excellent and to come to you when facing a fork in the road or an obstacle or when they need to reevaluate goals or resources. The best bosses I've ever had all led this way. They trusted me to do my job until I needed help, and then they trusted me to raise my hand and ask for help if I needed it."

Amen!

When you recruit talented employees and trust them to do the jobs they are hired to do, they will hold themselves accountable to you, their coworkers, and, most importantly, themselves. So delegate, give them the support they need, and trust them to get the work done, even when it's hard and uncomfortable. And when they mess up, which will happen, use it as an opportunity for them to learn and grow.

LITTLE THINGS CAN BE A BIG DEAL

Some things in our culture often mattered more to our employees than we realized. Pay attention to the things that may seem minor to you but are a big deal to your team members.

When we moved into our new office in 2009, I (Kass) didn't see the need to spend money on eighty-plus individual phone lines for each employee. iPhones, introduced the same year we launched Buddy Media, were now widely used by most of our team members. But when I set up shared group desk phones, it caused a bit of a stink. OK, it was a pretty big stink. There was something about having a phone on their desk that made them feel important—and something about not having it that made them feel less important.

The same thing happened with what I affectionately call "Staplegate." Along with other office essentials, we gave employees a certain kind of stapler during their onboarding process. When that product was discontinued, however, our HR team found a new one we could buy in bulk for less. The employees who got the new staplers thought they somehow were missing out. Our cultural glue became less sticky because people didn't like their staplers!

The point, as Spencer Johnson illustrated so creatively decades ago, is that moving even a tiny piece of cheese can cause significant stress on your culture.[*] [†] Entrepreneurs quickly adapt to change. Many of us are addicted to it, which is why we are often trying to destroy the status quo. Some of your employees, however, will find even the most minor change hard. Think through the implications of anything that will shape or modify how employees work together in your cult. And when you walk in one morning to an office full of crap that resulted from something you didn't anticipate being a big deal, remember it's your job to listen, care, own it, and shovel it.

CUTTING THROUGH THE CRAP: KEY LESSONS LEARNED

- Your job as the founder is to lead by example, including making hard and often unpopular decisions.
- Use compensation (competitive salaries, ownership plans, and effective reviews) to align employees' interests with the company's mission.
- Promote from within when possible, provided you see someone doing their job *and* leading their team.
- Clarify and communicate your roles and those of everyone in the company.
- Cultivate an empowerment culture by transparently sharing information.
- Build trust by owning your mistakes.

---

[*] *Who Moved My Cheese?* by Spencer Johnson is a short business fable first published in 1998 and is one of my (Kass's) favorite books on change management.

[†] Johnson, Spencer. *Who Moved My Cheese?* G.P. Putnam's Sons, 1998.

- Be mindful that even small changes are challenging for many.

PERCEPTION IS REALITY

THE CRAP THAT COMES WITH MARKETING FOR SUCCESS.

Liquid Death founder Mike Cessario never lets product feedback leave a bad taste in his mouth. So when one online hater said he would "rather lick sweat off a fat guy's back than drink Liquid Death," Mike decided to run his own blind taste test to find out which tasted better.

On one side of the "Better Than Back Sweat Official Taste Test" was Liquid Death's popular canned waters and teas. On the other was the real back sweat of comedian Zack "Zackass" Holmes, a prodigious perspirator notorious for his role in the *Jackass* movies.

Regular people licked the sweat off of Zackass's back, and ten out of ten preferred Liquid Death to the sweat. Like many of the company's humorous pieces, the video spread fast online as fans drank it up and shared it with their friends.

If you didn't happen to catch the sweat test, you may have seen the video promoting the Liquid Death Enema from the Enema of the State Collectible Kit featuring Travis Barker, the heavily tattooed drummer for Blink-182. Or the one with Martha Stewart in the kitchen holding a cleaver while promoting her Dismembered Moments Luxury Candle in the shape of a human hand holding a can of Liquid Death. "It is so realistic," the video says, "that you and your guests might wonder just how Martha made them."

Liquid Death made the candles and the enema kits and offered them for sale online. Both sold out quickly, and the enema kit is now trading on eBay for nearly twice the original retail price of 182 dollars.

Zackass is not the only one sweating. Liquid Death's irreverent ads, healthy products, and commitment to donating a portion of every sale to remove plastic from the oceans has other beverage companies perspiring over the prospect of lost profits. Five years after it sold its first can, Liquid Death is available in more than 113,000 retail locations. The company generated $263 million in retail sales in 2023, posting triple-digit growth for the third consecutive year, and it was the fastest-growing brand in both water and iced teas categories, according to industry data provider SPINS.[*]

Few entrepreneurs have taken a more counterintuitive approach than Mike Cessario, a former punk rocker turned creative director. The product name came from brainstorming the "dumbest possible name for a super-healthy"[†] beverage and then testing its resonance with an online video before the product was created.

---

[*] "Liquid Death Closes $67 Million in Strategic Financing Including Top Distributors at $1.4 Billion Valuation." *Business Wire,* March 11, 2024. https://www.businesswire.com/news/home/20240310837019/en/Liquid-Death-closes-67-million-in-strategic-financing-including-top-distributors-at-1.4-billion-valuation.

[†] Huddleston, Tom and Zachary Green. "How Liquid Death's 40-Year-Old Founder Turned 'the Dumbest Name' and a Facebook Post into a $700 Million Water Brand." *CNBC,* November 26, 2022. https://www.cnbc.com/2022/11/26/liquid-death-ceo-mike-cessario-we-chose-the-dumbest-possible-name-for-water.html.

As two of Mike's earliest investors and advisors, we are often asked about the company and why we got involved way before it was clear that the water-in-a-can-with-a-dumb-name startup would develop a cult-like following of thirst murderers.

Our friends Peter Pham and Mike Jones at Los Angeles-based venture studio Science, Inc., which helped incubate Liquid Death, introduced us to the company. While we don't normally get involved with consumer packaged-goods companies, this one grabbed our attention because Science had incubated Dollar Shave Club, which Unilever bought for about $1 billion as one of its first direct-to-consumer acquisitions.

When we evaluated Mike's original idea through our Go Gauge, it tasted refreshingly great—a differentiated product in a huge market with great unit economics at scale. One other factor, however, convinced us to provide some initial seed capital: we knew Mike, a former creative director at Gary Vaynerchuk's agency, VaynerMedia, would market like no other founder we had ever worked with.

We share his story often because inside Mike's marketing strategy are lessons for all entrepreneurs, regardless of industry, opportunity, or company stage.

Mike's dream started when he scored a backstage pass for the 2009 Vans Warped Tour music festival in Denver. He noticed that many punk band members on stage were drinking water from Monster Energy drink cans. Monster Energy was their sponsor but not their beverage of choice.

Why aren't there more healthy products with fun, cool, irreverent branding? he asked himself. *Why do the only companies that push the marketing limits sell toxic products—fast food, beer, chips, candy bars, and sugar-filled energy drinks?*

Mike landed on water as his perfect category—a large market ($300 billion-plus in 2022[*]) ripe for a challenger brand that planned to use cool and exciting marketing to stick out.

Liquid Death was trademarked in 2017 and launched in 2019. Mike thought the name, in bold gothic font above the artistic skull on a tallboy can, would make people lean in to learn more (and smile, take a photo, and post it to their social accounts.) And its tagline, "Death to Plastic," emphasizes its efforts to remove plastic from the environment, a cause that would resonate with young consumers.

The naysayers said the product packaging would confuse shoppers and that retailers would never stock it with "death" in the name. (This would also become a concern of ours in 2020. Can we really sell "death water" during a global pandemic?)

Fast-forward to 2024 and investors rewarded the company's performance with a $1.4 billion valuation in its most recent financing round. As Amazon's number one water brand, it is now the most promising challenger brand in the massive water market.

Not bad for a company that has bought the souls of 225,000 customers and counting![†] (You can sell yours to Liquid Death in exchange for membership to the Liquid Death Country Club on the company's website. Beware, though! The agreement is binding and commits your soul to Liquid Death "to the ends of the earth

---

[*] "Bottled Water Market Size." *Grand View Research,* accessed August 7, 2024. https://www.grandviewresearch.com/industry-analysis/bottled-water-market.

[†] Stone, Sam. "How Liquid Death Became Gen Z's La Croix." *Bon Appétit*, October 29, 2022. https://www.bonappetit.com/story/liquid-death-canned-water-gen-z.

and for the rest of time [including, without limitation, any applicable afterlife, reincarnation or similar post-mortal existence]."*)

It's all in good fun, which is Mike's strategy.

"We don't want to create a marketing company," Mike said during a CNBC interview. "We want to actually entertain people and make them laugh in service to a brand. If we can do that, they're going to love [our] brand, because [we] are giving them something of value."[†]

Whether or not you are also on an "evil mission . . . to make people laugh and get more of them to drink more healthy beverages more often, all while helping to kill plastic pollution,"[‡] it's hard to argue that Liquid Death isn't darn good marketing.

MAKE MARKETING MATTER

While Buddy Media's tactics differed greatly from Liquid Death's, the marketing principles were similar. Buddy Media took off by selling a software tool for social media marketing and used humor and fun as key pillars of our marketing and to support our company culture.

Marketing is essential to entrepreneurial success. Take a great idea for a product, throw a barrel of money at development, and

---

* "Soul Contract." *Liquid Death*, accessed August 7, 2024. https://liquiddeath.com/pages/soul-contract.

† Huddleston, Tom and Zachary Green. "How Liquid Death's 40-Year-Old Founder Turned 'the Dumbest Name' and a Facebook Post into a $700 Million Water Brand." *CNBC*, November 26, 2022. https://www.cnbc.com/2022/11/26/liquid-death-ceo-mike-cessario-we-chose-the-dumbest-possible-name-for-water.html.

‡ "Manifesto." *Liquid Death,* accessed August 7, 2024. https://liquiddeath.com/pages/manifesto.

then keep it a secret from the world. Guess what happens? Nothing. No one buys it because no one knows about it.

You don't have to shock the world with a brilliantly "dumb" name or ads worthy of *Saturday Night Live,* but you also can't sit on your hands and expect the reality you want for your company to materialize magically.

There's simply no excuse for failing to invest in marketing. It doesn't take tons of money to promote a product or service. Liquid Death invested a few thousand dollars on its first online ad, and in the month when it had its first $100,000 in sales, the company spent only about $2,000 on marketing.*

They did have a clearly defined marketing plan for telling the world about Liquid Death. What's your plan for your company?

BUILD A COMPREHENSIVE BRAND STRATEGY

Building a brand is more than just creating a logo and tagline. A comprehensive marketing plan consists of three legs of the marketing stool: developing your brand strategy, creating your brand identity, and executing your brand marketing.

Too many companies just want to do "fun marketing"—brand identity (building a logo). But you need to focus on all three aspects of marketing. If any leg is weak, you don't want to be the one sitting on the stool.

---

* Huddleston, Tom and Zachary Green. "How Liquid Death's 40-Year-Old Founder Turned 'the Dumbest Name' and a Facebook Post into a $700 Million Water Brand." *CNBC*, November 26, 2022. https://www.cnbc.com/2022/11/26/liquid-death-ceo-mike-cessario-we-chose-the-dumbest-possible-name-for-water.html.

Buddy Media was entering a new industry, and we eventually had about a hundred funded social media marketing competitors (at our last count!). We needed to stand out—with our name, what we stood for, our messages, and how we took those messages to the world.

We hired Katherine Bateman of Kayelbee Associates within the first week of starting the company because I (Kass) knew the importance of quickly creating a comprehensive marketing plan, starting with the first leg of developing our brand strategy.

For a startup, this marketing plan becomes the blueprint for growing the business into a lasting brand and provides guidelines for all teams and departments, regardless of the number of employees on your payroll.

As investors, we're often approached by startups with a name and a logo but that haven't thought through their messaging, especially as it compares to their competitors. Worse, some have moved forward with a name and logo but haven't done a comprehensive trademark search. The money and time are wasted when they have to start all over on their brand. Or they constantly change their messages in the first few months based on their latest sales call and end up without a unified, cohesive message for anyone, let alone their target audience.

Thinking through every marketing phase from the beginning will serve you well in the long run. You will need to change it over time, but you can do so intentionally and without falling off your stool.

BUILD A LASTING BRAND

The goal of your brand strategy (Phase 1) is to build a brand that withstands your company's twists and turns. The work you have already done upfront to greenlight the business and find your first customers will give you a head start. But it requires you to know very specific information.

Know your product—What's different and what's unique? Liquid Death was water in a can, not plastic bottles. Buddy Media was a software as a service that helped big brands reach their audiences on major social media platforms.

Know your benefits—Don't just identify features (attributes like the camera in an iPhone); talk about benefits and advantages to the customer like how an iPhone makes taking photos simple and fun.

Benefits can be expressed in what your product does for customers, but also—and often—in how your brand makes them feel. For instance, the benefit of buying Liquid Death is that you can hydrate and remove plastics from the ocean in the process. That's a powerful story that resonates with shoppers—far more shoppers, as it turned out, than Mike Cessario expected.

Every company, not just consumer brands, should create a brand that resonates with its core buyers. Few companies have truly unique products. Outside of a few categories, most of us don't buy because of the features and functions; we buy because of the brand's meaning, how it makes us feel, and what the brand says about our identity.

Liquid Death may or may not taste better than other brands, although we can definitively say (based on Mike's research, not our personal experience) that it tastes better than the sweat from the back of Zackass Holmes. But it makes people laugh and feel cool and is better for the environment.

Know your audience—Who are you selling to? What are their demographics (gender, age, income, etc.)? What are their psychographics (belief systems, values, attitudes)? How many are there (total available market—or TAM)? And what are their pain points?

Know your competitors—What are they offering? How do they differ from you? How is their offering better than yours? Do your homework (a SWOT analysis and a competitor analysis are good tools to use).

The more you know, the better equipped you are to create simple messaging that you can apply consistently to everything you produce, from pitch decks to live client pitches to branded collateral to advertisements. Consistency with your messages is the *only* way to build your brand.

When you align what your brand does well with what your customer really wants and what your competition doesn't offer, you can identify your Unique Selling Proposition (USP), that sweet spot where your benefits are truly unique and defensible, and you have a great answer for the critical question from your customer: "What's in this brand for me?"

A brand strategy that lives in this sweet spot will have stable legs and last for many years, adapting and growing even if you have to pivot your business model, add a new revenue stream, or battle new competitors who enter your space.

DON'T OVERVALUE THE LOGO AND MARK

During Phase 2, building your brand identity, it's pretty common to invest a lot of initial time and money on the colors, fonts, patterns, and icons for a logo and mark that go on business cards (woo-hoo!) and other collateral material, eventually getting to the website. While you want these to be good, there's a tendency to overemphasize the brand identity phase.

A company's brand identity begins with its name. We settled on the name Buddy Media because of its reference to friends. And we owned the domain name, buddymedia.com, which we acquired as part of the acquisition of Aryeh Goldsmith's applications. (Other domains we bought included idatedhim.com, buddyboy.com, and metabuddy.com.) We didn't like the name Buddy Media. Our head of brand marketing Katherine Bateman really didn't like it, either. But she taught us to focus on things that were far more important. She was right.

Instead of taking six months to find a new name that could be trademarked (close to impossible to do) with a matching URL (even harder to do) and then creating a whole new identity, we hit the ground running with the less-than-ideal name and URL we already had. If we had re-branded, we would have lost that time to our competitors, and Katherine convinced us that it was more important to go to market and protect the crap out of the brand we already had than to waste time coming up with a new "perfect" name and logo.

CREATING A REALITY WITH PERCEPTION (KASS)

"Perception is reality," coined in 1988 by political strategist Lee Atwater, is a phrase that came to define how we think about brand marketing within our companies. But it was a concept I first learned at Jaffe when I set out to build the firm's interactive arm.

At first, I couldn't imagine we could get paid much money to build websites. Law firm websites then included a general overview, contact information, and a list of partners' names. I soon realized that websites were the perfect way to elevate the image of the firms we worked with.

A robust site turned the firms into publishers and thought leaders who shared the latest developments from their practice areas with content written by their most accomplished lawyers. They could share their big wins and show they were forward-looking and innovative without saying it outright.

Today, a website is a basic requirement for companies. But the concept—using marketing to create the perception that you are bigger than you are—is just as important today as it was when I built my first law firm website. Technology and tactics have changed but the strategy is the same.

When you have completed your strategy (Phase 1) and your brand identity (Phase 2) and moved to implementation (Phase 3), it's time to act bigger than you are, especially in a nascent industry with many smaller competitors. Fake it until you make it—but in a much bigger way.

For example, in late 2010, KB and her team created and executed (flawlessly, I might add) an airport advertising campaign that loudly and proudly staked Buddy Media's claim as the leader in our space (even though that wasn't necessarily the case yet).

Our tactic of making a big splash by using airport ads was an idea that our board loved—but only after it proved successful. When I first recommended a $1 million addition to our marketing budget, however, it went over like a crap sandwich. The reaction from our board: "Are you out of your mind?!"

After considerable debate, most of it heated, the board agreed, and the plan went forward. We knew the company, competitors, and space better than anyone on our board and fought hard for what we thought would catapult us into the lead.

We launched the campaign on the Monday before Thanksgiving and it ran through Martin Luther King Day in January 2011. The billboards were prominent in the three major airports serving New York City and also in Seattle, San Francisco, Los Angeles, Cincinnati, and Chicago. We modeled the copy on ideas I used years earlier at Jaffe when marketing my dad's law firm.

"7 OF THE WORLD'S TOP 10 BRANDS BUILD THEIR BUSINESS ON FACEBOOK WITH OUR TOOLS," our ads screamed. Then came a simple question—"What's your plan?"—and the link to our website.

We also delivered a one-two punch by placing full-page ads with the same messaging on the front and back covers of *AdAge* and *Adweek*, the two biggest marketing industry trade magazines. We knew the decision-makers of large brands (our target audience) would travel at some point from Thanksgiving through New Year's, and we would hit them over the head with our messaging—whether they were walking through an airport or catching up on the latest industry news.

The campaign helped create the perception that Buddy Media was bigger than it was. That perception became our reality and powered our growth. As an added benefit, many of our ad spots weren't sold after our contract expired the following year. Since traditional billboards had not yet been replaced by the digital screens widely used today, our advertising stayed up for several more months—almost a year in some airports.

The growth after the campaign was enormous. We can't attribute it all to the brand marketing, but we know it was the spark. In the quarter following the campaign, total sales were up 300 percent to $9.8 million, annual recurring revenue had also tripled to $18 million from $6 million a year earlier, and average deal size had doubled in a year to $75,000 per customer.

The campaign also became a source of massive pride within the company. Buddies beamed when they traveled for the holidays, taking pictures and sharing with everyone on social media.

The concept of promoting the reality you are creating should influence everything you do and everyone involved in your company—investors, board members, employees, and partners, as well as customers.

This isn't about shining a turd. It's about using the right facts to create the perception that you are equal to or better than your largest competitors. In the same way that a boxer sometimes fights competition in a heavier weight class, startups need to punch above their weight with their brand marketing. Your advertising should never be about (or mention) smaller competitors; instead, go after the bigger incumbents with a dominant market share.

You can do this successfully by selectively displaying statistics in your ads. Our airport ads emphasized that we worked with the world's top companies, not our revenue figures or market share.

We also learned that by strategically picking our marketing opportunities, we could do more with less.

One area where we found that to be particularly true was conferences and sponsorships. Since Kass handled the company operations and most of the hands-on care with our children, I (Mike) ended up as the public face of our companies and handled most of the writing and speaking opportunities that set me up as an industry thought leader.

KB never tried to just get a speaking gig for me, nor did she try to just sponsor an event, like a dinner at a conference. Instead, she sought opportunities to sponsor the conference where I spoke. This doubled our impact and increased our brand presence. We concentrated our spending but owned all of it, and our brand hit attendees from all angles—advertising around the speaking engagement *and* the opportunity to speak about what Buddy Media could do for the customers in the audience.

At SXSW in 2012, we owned only two unique things. First, we wrapped the stairs at the Austin airport with our new ad campaign so everyone saw it when they arrived and departed. Second, we served coffee to attendees in branded Buddy Media cups from branded golf carts. This turned out particularly well because that year was miserably cold and rainy. Our brand marketing tactic was both memorable and impactful.

Like Liquid Death, Buddy Media was different. We stood out. We didn't market like most software companies. We marketed like the world-class brand we thought we were. This helped Buddy Media survive and grow, especially early on when we had to face one of our biggest questions: death or pivot?

CUTTING THROUGH THE CRAP: KEY LESSONS LEARNED

- Invest early in a unified brand—build a comprehensive marketing plan that consists of your brand strategy, your brand identity, and executing your brand marketing.
- Know your product, benefits, audience, and competition to get to your Unique Selling Proposition—the sweet spot for sharing your offering with your target audience.

- Don't overvalue your logo or mark. Instead, emphasize getting to market and protecting your brand.
- In the beginning, act bigger than you are because perception is reality.
- Don't spread your marketing dollars too thin; own one event rather than a little bit of many events.
- Look for ways to stand out by marketing differently.

DEATH AND THE PIVOT
THE ENTREPRENEUR'S ULTIMATE CRAP-SHOVELING EXERCISE.

The SXSW Conference in Austin, Texas, is a weeklong celebration of culture, education, music, film, and tech. I (Mike) have been a regular attendee and speaker since Buddy Media's early days. It's always enlightening and memorable, but never more so than in March 2011.

Gary Vaynerchuk was hosting one of his infamous "jam sessions." Instead of hitting one of the bars on Austin's Sixth Street or attending the always-raucous Foursquare party, Gary convened a handful of friends in his hotel suite to talk about the future of the internet business. In addition to Gary and me, the group included Travis Kalanick (the founder of Uber, who was in town to launch his car service in Austin), Aaron Batalion (a wicked-smart engineer who started Groupon competitor Living Social), and Kevin Systrom (Instagram's cofounder).

Twitter's explosive launch at SXSW in 2007 turned SXSW into ground zero for early social app innovation. By 2011 the frenzy was in full force. So, it wasn't surprising that Gary quickly steered the conversation to the big social platforms.

All eyes turned to Kevin, a tall, boyish-looking Stanford grad sitting in the suite's main living room. Less than six months earlier, Kevin and his partner Mike Krieger had launched Instagram, and the app was now a white-hot challenger to MySpace, Facebook, Twitter, and LinkedIn, the largest social networks at the time. Gary, an early Facebook investor, asked Kevin whether he could compete with the big guys.

Kevin, who had turned down an offer from Mark Zuckerberg to join Facebook in 2006, was so confident he could compete that he said he would never sell the company to one of the larger platforms when it took off. Gary, the ultimate trader and gamer, laughed, knowing everything had a price.

Most people don't know that Instagram started as Burbn, Kevin's side project to learn coding. In this gamified version of the popular location app Foursquare, launched at SXSW two years earlier, users earned points for checking into local businesses. But the app was complicated, and very few people signed up for Burbn. Most who did never returned. It was dead on arrival.

Kevin could have folded and returned to his job as a product developer at a Bay Area startup. But he didn't give up. As Michael Dell says, "There's a simple part of this, which is, you just don't quit."[*]

---

[*] Lev-Ram, Michal, and Nicholas Gordon. "Michael Dell, Who's Led His Company for 40 Years, Shares the 'Simple' Secret to His Longevity." *Fortune*, March 25, 2024. https://fortune.com/2024/03/25/michael-dell-technologies-ceo-founder-longevity/.

One of the most promising Burbn features allowed users to post pictures with friends from any location on the app. Kevin, an avid photographer, believed this was unique (it was!) and would resonate with users as a standalone app (it did!). He stripped everything from the Burbn app except the ability for a user to add a filter to a photo, post the photo, like a photo, and comment on a post.

He named the app Instagram.

With an iconic, nostalgia-infused logo inspired by Polaroid's instant photography, Instagram became a place to immortalize your best shots online where anyone could see them, like them, and comment on them in real time. It combined the best of Polaroid (instant results sans darkroom) with the best of Facebook (frictionless tagging and sharing among friends), striking a chord with people worldwide just as mobile phones put a quality camera in each of our pockets.

Later that year, Apple named Instagram the iPhone App of the Year. A year after he told us he wouldn't sell, Facebook purchased Kevin's thirteen-person company for $1 billion in cash and stock. Instagram is now one of the most recognized brands on the planet, and Kevin is one of the most successful and respected entrepreneurs I know—and quite rich thanks to the growth of the Facebook stock he received.

THE PIVOT PROCESS

Kevin's results were unique. His process was not.

Even if you know the problem you are trying to solve, have deep industry knowledge, and are armed with mounds of customer survey data, creating a product at an acceptable price point and landing customers is no easy feat. Most new companies don't get it right the first or even the second time.

You have three options if things aren't turning out as you expected. You can continue doing more of what isn't working, fold the business, or stop doing what's not working, create a new plan, and change direction. The last option is called a pivot, a term popularized in business by Eric Ries in his 2011 best-selling book, *The Lean Startup*.

This is one of the most stressful leadership tasks an entrepreneur will face. Pivots involve creating and executing a new plan that often includes a team reorganization, layoffs, new hires, additional financing, new technology and priorities, and a new origin story. This is only after a leader has the insight, fearlessness, and humility to see that change is needed.

Leaders often learn the most, gain the most, and are judged the most during pivots. Growth and good times have a way of hiding issues. Pivots expose warts and require founders to have the courage, leadership skills, and finesse to bring others along with them through the change.

Insights and humility come from recognizing that you don't have all the answers, and from surrounding yourself with people you trust to tell you the uncomfortable truth, instead of a bunch of echo chamber sycophants. When you pivot, you must let go of the ego that keeps whispering (or screaming) that you need to keep moving in the wrong direction because you just *know* your original approach was right. For a pivot to succeed, many of the once-sacred cows in the company must be slaughtered. This is tough for most founders, especially those who let their pride dictate their decisions.

It seems logical to do less of what isn't working and more of what is working. But logic has no chance against pride or fear.

FOUNDER FEAR IS REAL

We have seen fear's destructive force wreak havoc on once-well-oiled operations that needed a new direction.

> *I can't switch to Y when I have raised money to do X.*
> *I don't have the skill sets at the company needed to pivot to Y.*
> *I will be ridiculed by the press if news of our pivot leaks.*
> *I can't lay off a great team that has finally gelled.*

All of these fear-based reactions lead to inaction and paralysis.

Fear is one of the most basic and powerful human emotions. Prehistoric entrepreneurs may not have understood much about how the world worked. But they understood fear. It compelled them to run from the wild beasts looking to eat them.

Ask founders what they worry about, and you will hear a relatively short list of other fears—fear of failure, fear of not being good enough, fear of letting others down, fear of rejection, fear of what others will think, fear of making a wrong decision, fear of having to work for someone else.

These fears are not all bad, like the fear that drives you to run from a bear looking for food. They can motivate you to work harder and dig deeper to keep your company alive and growing. Nonetheless, fear often leads to suboptimal decision-making. It is tough to make great decisions when you are riddled with fear. Fear and the distorted judgment it leaves in its wake are much more likely to kill your business than competition.

The fear of failure (which might result in a job working for someone else) and the fear of letting others down prevent entrepreneurs from taking the risks needed to grow their businesses.

The fear of not being good enough leads to inaction because you lack the confidence that you can make meaningful change happen.

The fear of what investors, mentors, and colleagues will think of you prevents you from seeking uncomfortable truths or advice on important decisions.

Fear of rejection leads to staying quiet about the problems you see rather than speaking up about the need for a new direction.

The fear of making the wrong decision leads to decision constipation, increasing the likelihood that you will miss your window of opportunity.

TAKING THE LEAP

Leading an organization through a pivot is like captaining a skydive. Both are scary, but when done well, can result in a fantastic experience.

Detailed planning, flawless execution, and deep trust among those jumping with you are mere starting points for a skydive captain. Even with everything in place, much can and does go wrong after you jump. Flying 120 miles per hour toward your destination—literally or figuratively!—with minimal protection never happens without fear.

A founder often needs to jump first and then build the company's parachute! Leading an organization through a pivot is not about convincing people to abandon their fears. It's getting people to jump alongside you, undeterred by their fear. If they sense you are scared or haven't thought through and clearly communicated the plan you are asking them to execute, they will never jump with you.

Like many emotions entrepreneurs encounter during their journey, fear is not one you can control or avoid. You can only control how you respond to it. And for your company, that response is often the difference between life (surviving and growing) and death (shrinking and going out of business).

Identify the fear. Address the elephant in the room. And make sure your decisions are not driven by fear.

We recognize that this is easier said than done for our fellow optimists and dreamers. I (Mike) ask one simple question to entrepreneurs grappling with making a decision they know in their gut is right: *what is the worst thing that can happen if you do this?* Typically, the worst-case scenario isn't that bad and beats the alternative (continuing to do what's not working and running out of money).

Courage to act comes from overcoming your fears, not getting rid of them. This now comes relatively easy for me and others like me who have lived through near-death experiences.

Before the heart surgeries that saved my life after nearly flatlining at my doctor's office when I was nineteen, many of my decisions were driven by fear. I was scared to ask out girls (fear of rejection). I was scared to eat with people I didn't know—fearful that I would get diarrhea or throw up, two byproducts of my weak stomach (fear of embarrassing myself). I was scared I would drop a flyball (fear of performing) and ended up quitting the baseball team my junior year of high school when the coach said I had to play the outfield.

After I almost died, I found myself asking again and again, "What's the worst thing that can happen?"

What's the worst thing that can happen if I ask Kass to dance?

What's the worst thing that can happen if I start a company and it fails?

What's the worst thing that can happen if we pivot Buddy Media from Acebucks to enterprise software?

If I fail, I fail. But if I try my best with integrity, there's not much else I can do.

REASONS TO PIVOT

You may need to pivot for many reasons. The initial market might be smaller than you thought. New opportunities might arise that you want to attack. A technology shift might make your product less attractive to customers. The government may issue new regulations that force you to change.

You may need to pivot into a new business model, target market, or pricing model. Or, like Kevin Systrom with Instagram, you might stay in the same space and alter your product to something better received by your customers.

Regardless of why or to what degree, if you need to pivot, then pivot. Rip the bandage off. The sooner you plan and do it, the quicker you will find yourself on your true path to success.

We should know. It took us three business models at Buddy Media to get it right!

Our initial model was building and monetizing our own games. We realized we were not the team to attack this space and pivoted into Acebucks, which provided apps and other businesses on Facebook with a loyalty-based point system. We quickly discovered companies had no interest in Acebucks but were very interested in launching their own social media marketing. We pivoted into enterprise software, and Buddy Media's fun began!

And by fun, we mean chaos and trauma followed by a mild case of PTSD. At least to some degree.

We had to completely rethink our entire company, which caused me (Kass) to go through a mini meltdown. When I think about the fear I experienced driven by that change, the feelings still come rushing back as if I were going through it again.

While discussing the shift to a SaaS company during a board meeting, I had to leave the conference room to avoid a panic attack in front of everyone. I knew the board, especially Mike, was right (recurring revenue = good). But I also knew everything would have to change—not just how our product was built, but how our teams were organized, how processes were implemented, how we communicated with clients, and whether we needed all the people we had on the payroll.

Pivots are *hard* operationally.

If you are launching a service business (accounting, legal, staffing, etc.), you may never need to pivot. But if you are doing something new, there is a very good chance a pivot (or two) will be required. Almost every company we have started or funded, other than Walter Driver's Scopely, has pivoted at some point. If your gut says you need to pivot, you are not alone.

Slack was an internal tool used by the gaming company Tiny Speck during the development of an online game called Glitch. While Glitch failed, Slack evolved into the leading platform for team collaboration.

When YouTube launched on Valentine's Day 2005, its slogan was "Tune In, Hook Up." Only after failing miserably as a video dating company did the founders launch the user-generated video site. YouTube is now the most popular video site on the internet.

Pivoting as a larger company is often more important and even more fear-inducing. Turning a row boat is easy. Turning a freighter stacked with shipping containers is not.

Some of the greatest companies you know have pivoted many times since they were founded. They are a product of the decisions made by fearless leaders, all of whom had far-from-perfect data. But they had respected leaders, money in the bank, and the courage to initiate bold changes.

Sony would be the world's largest rice cooker manufacturer today if founder Tokyo Tsushin Kogyo had not recognized the growing global demand for innovative technology. Introducing the TR-55 transistor radio set Sony on its path as a pioneer in electronic goods. Sony's market cap is now more than $100 billion.

Bayerische Flugzeugwerke AG manufactured aircraft engines during World War I, but the Treaty of Versailles forced it to stop. The company shifted to motorcycle production in 1923 and automobile manufacturing in 1928 before launching a "New Class" sedan while on the brink of bankruptcy in the early 1960s. The company, which changed its name to Bayerische Motoren Werke, or BMW, went on to develop the iconic BMW 3 Series.

We spent many weekend evenings watching DVDs when we lived in Chicago while building Golf.com. Chicago winters are cold. So, we signed up right away when Netflix began offering a mail-order DVD rental service, eliminating our trips to Lincoln Park's Blockbuster store (helpful during blizzards). It was a novel concept that challenged traditional video rental stores.

The largest chain at the time, Blockbuster, served more than sixty-five million customers through its nine thousand physical stores. The model was simple: Blockbuster bought movies from the studio for about $65 and rented them out—up to $5 per rental for the latest movies and $2 for older titles. If you were late returning the movie, you would be charged a penalty ($1 for each delinquent day).

In one year, Blockbuster raked in over $800 million dollars' worth of late fees (about half must have been from us, and by us, we mean Mike)!

Netflix had three major benefits: it had a better selection, was more convenient, and customers paid no late fees. Netflix's DVD-by-mail service was a huge hit, reaching ten million subscribers and more than $10 billion in revenue by 2010. Netflix founder Reed Hastings was on top of the world, or so it seemed. But something in his gut wasn't feeling right. He just didn't see how his business would not be severely impacted by faster internet speeds and consumers expecting instant gratification through the internet. Nothing screams slow like the United States Postal Service he used to deliver his DVDs to his customers!

Reed started pivoting the organization with a small special-ops team even though his DVD-by-mail business was still three years from its peak. On Valentine's Day 2007, Netflix launched its initial foray into streaming by giving DVD customers about a thousand titles they could download via the internet and watch on their computers. The same month, the company sent out its billionth DVD!

This was not an easy decision to make. Internet infrastructure at the time could not support a streaming service at scale. Netflix investors were concerned about the capital outlay required to build its own infrastructure to support the new offering and the expensive licensing deals they would need to make with the movie studios. Netflix was marginally profitable at the time (about $50 million in annual profits), and the move would lower the company's profit in the foreseeable future.

Netflix announced its $7.99-a-month streaming service in 2010, decoupling internet delivery from the mail delivery option for the first time. (Blockbuster, which had laughed off an offer to buy Netflix for $50 million in 2000, filed for bankruptcy the same year.) And with the production of its *House of Cards* show in 2013, Netflix was no longer just a content distributor. It had also pivoted into being a major content creator and owner and has done more to shape the landscape of modern television and film than anyone since my grandfather's early partners, the brothers Warner.

In September 2023, sixteen years after its initial pivot into streaming began, Netflix shipped its final DVD (its five billionth!). The results of its many pivots speak for themselves—if you had bought $10,000 of Netflix stock at the February 14, 2007, streaming launch, it would be worth about $1.8 million today.

Netflix's destiny as a DVD rental service would have been the same as Blockbuster, the company it helped kill, if not for a leader who listened to his gut and was brave enough to pivot to a streaming service and then a content engine. More importantly, Netflix's story warns all leaders to embrace "change and pivot, or die."

TRUST YOUR GUT

As entrepreneurs with a reputation for innovating, leaders often ask us how they can reach the future faster. When we speak to company leaders of all sizes about pivots, one word comes up repeatedly—a word we have already used multiple times in this chapter—your gut.

You rarely find the inspiration for a pivot from management consultants, advisers, or board members. The pivot usually starts deep inside you. You feel something. You have an intuition that something is wrong or there's an opportunity ahead that should command your attention. You have an itch asking to be scratched.

Tune into your gut. That feeling you get deep down in your belly is usually right. Rarely have we heard someone say they shouldn't have listened to their gut or that their gut gets them in trouble.

It's the opposite—your gut embodies the output of your subconscious processing all the structured and unstructured data around you: your company's data, industry data, economic data, what experts are saying and not saying, the uncomfortable truths.

You may recognize the following pattern. You have a gut feeling about something. You then spend two weeks trying to talk yourself out of that feeling only to realize suddenly maybe it's too late and you should have listened to your gut from the beginning.

Save yourself the time and pain. If you feel you should pivot, regardless of company size or reason, tune into it, create a clear plan, and make the changes when you are healthy and have time. Then don't look back. Move forward confidently and market what you have aggressively because perception is reality.

Until, that is, your gut tells you it's time for another pivot!

CUTTING THROUGH THE CRAP: KEY LESSONS LEARNED

- When your company needs a change, you have three options: continue doing what you've been doing, fold your business, or pivot.
- Leading a company through a pivot requires insight, fearlessness, and humility.

- If a pivot is necessary and you struggle with fears, ask yourself one question: what's the worst thing that can happen if you do this?
- Getting people to follow you during a pivot isn't about convincing them to abandon their fears. It's about getting them to work with and believe in you despite the fear.
- Recognizing the need to pivot almost always begins with trusting your gut.

EXIT

THE FLOWERS THAT COME FROM LOVING THE SHOVEL.

We know hundreds of entrepreneurs. We have partnered with them, competed against them, and invested with and in them for decades. And, thanks to our time at Salesforce, we have learned from our generation's most iconic software entrepreneur, Marc Benioff.

As investors, we spend much of our days providing founders with support. Often it starts with helping them think through the crap that keeps them up at night—fundraisings, hires, layoffs, employee and legal issues, and, of course, pivots.

Invariably, the conversations move to a deeper—and typically darker—level. When asked how their companies are doing, founders almost always say "great" or "we're crushing it." But get a founder alone for a coffee or meal, and they will talk about the toll shoveling in the dark with no guarantee of treasure has taken on their physical and emotional health and personal relationships.

I (Mike) have met no entrepreneur who better represents the dichotomy between crushing it and getting crushed than Tony Hsieh, the former CEO of Zappos, the online retailer once widely recognized as the "Happiest Company" on earth.

After Zappos sold to Amazon in 2009 for $1.2 billion, Tony turned much of his attention to revitalizing downtown Las Vegas. While still serving as CEO of Zappos (until 2020), Tony launched the Downtown Project, his boldest company and the first that he started alone. Funded with an initial investment of $350 million, Tony's goal was to turn Vegas's downtown into the happiest community on the planet by applying the customer-focused approach outlined in his best-selling book *Delivering Happiness* to urban planning.

Tony was creating a city as a startup, using real estate acquisitions and development as the engine. He envisioned the most community-focused large city in the world—a place where everything you needed and wanted was within walking distance.

I felt Tony's passion for that vision the last time we were together. It was January 2019, and Tony's beloved Vegas Golden Knights had just lost a heartbreaker to the San Jose Sharks. Up 2-1 in the third period, the Knights gave up a pair of goals thirty-nine seconds apart and lost the game. But Tony was in a good mood. And when Tony was feeling good, his happiness was contagious. My friend and Liquid Death co-investor, Peter Pham, and I laughed with Tony in his Golden Knights-branded tour bus in the parking lot outside the VIP entrance of the T-Mobile Arena.

Life seemed good for Tony. Little did I know what was happening under the surface.

Tony's mission in life was to create happiness, and he succeeded, especially when creating happiness for others. Employees loved working for him, and everyone loved being around him. Tony was a born founder. But years of struggling to bring his latest and largest vision to life followed by the COVID-19 lockdown crushed Tony's mental health.

Less than two years after we sat together on his bus, Tony died from what the coroner called "complications from smoke inhalation," locked in a small room surrounded by candles in a Connecticut home blaze.

Tony was unusually talented and magnetic, but his struggles with the pressures of a life spent focused on accomplishing a huge and complicated mission were not unusual. His story serves as a warning about the difficulties that are common to anyone who spends a large chunk of their lives shoveling crap. Entrepreneurs are self-selecting innovators, risk-takers, and dreamers. The identities of their companies merge with their identities as individuals. The constant barrage of the good and the bad—often on the same day—takes its toll.

It's a toll we know all too well. But it's a toll we don't regret paying. Because in the end, it was always about the love, not the crap.

PAYING OUR TOLL (MIKE)

I sat in Marc Benioff's townhouse on May 8, 2012, on the edge of the Presidio in one of San Francisco's ritziest neighborhoods, discussing Salesforce's interest in acquiring Buddy Media. It should have been an exciting and joyous day.

Facebook was planning to list its shares on the New York Stock Exchange the next week, which would allow us to realize the value of our early small investment in the company and validate our choice of

Facebook as Buddy Media's first and most important partner platform. And even though we were planning to take Buddy Media public on the NASDAQ stock exchange, we were also receiving acquisition interest from Salesforce, Yahoo, Google, and Microsoft.

Still in workout gear, Marc sat across from me at his conference table in a converted dining room, eating an energy bar. Like many great entrepreneurs we have met, Marc is a hands-on builder and leader. He wanted to experience, feel, and understand the product, so I opened my laptop and pulled up our social publishing and advertising software.

The software was easy to demo. With a few clicks, I uploaded a sample ad to our software, selected from dozens of Facebook targeting options (place of work, interests, colleges attended), highlighted areas on a map to geo-target the ads, and then launched the campaign.

I immediately knew Marc thought our software was cool. Marc and I share a common trait—when we get excited, you know it immediately. It is physically impossible to hide our enthusiasm.

Meanwhile, I noticed my mind drifting back to New York City, where my family struggled. Our oldest, Myles, was working through a health issue. Cole was getting in trouble at his school (he was bored). Vivi was with parents who could barely keep their own heads above water.

My constant travel had made it hard for Kass and me to stay connected. There's only so much connecting you can do from different time zones. Oh, and I had adopted a puppy, which I thought Kass would love because it was cute, even though she had only agreed to an adult rescue. Talk about shoveling shit—literally!

At work, we had just hired leadership coach Tammy Jersey, whose stated purpose was: "helping leaders rise to new levels of greatness." We asked her to evaluate the performances of the entire leadership team, including mine. And after talking to our leadership team, Tammy delivered a report that showed how much I needed to grow.

This was work I wanted to do, but it hurts when people you love to work with say stuff like, "At times, his comments and tone during senior-level meetings are more attacks on members of the management team and less thoughtful direction or criticism to move the company forward. I'm not sure he realizes that people are intimidated to approach him or that he's not a great listener."

Tammy confirmed I was broken, or at least very off my game. I felt like a failed dad, an unreliable husband, an absent friend, and I now had confirmation that I wasn't the business leader I hoped or thought I was. On the outside, I was crushing it. Inside, I was an emotional mess, and I wanted to run away from it all.

It didn't help that I could feel every one of the twenty pounds I had gained in the five years since starting Buddy Media. A year earlier I had stopped working out and I was embarrassed by my weight gain and scared about what it meant for my heart and artificial valve.

After meeting with Marc, I caught a flight for a reunion with my best friends from high school. They had invited me to Cabo to relax and blow off the stink for a weekend. Yes, I realize I was leaving on a "me trip" when Kass and I should have both been going. But this trip had been planned for months. Selfishly, I needed fun and downtime, neither of which lasted long.

On my first day in Mexico, while on the sixteenth hole of the El Dorado Golf Course, I got a call from John Somorjai, the head of Salesforce's corporate development team. John is one of the great unsung heroes of enterprise software and built the machine that is Salesforce's corporate development and venture investing teams. He walked me through the most important offer of our business careers as I scribbled notes on a golf scorecard.

Salesforce wanted to buy Buddy Media for close to a billion dollars. I should have been thrilled. But I went numb. The number was hard for me to digest. Kass and I had spent very little time thinking about an exit, and now generation-changing money was right in front of me.

I immediately left the course, called Kass, and spent the rest of the trip holed up in my room on calls with our board of directors, lawyers, and advisors. I also worked the phones to get the other suitors (Google, Microsoft, and Yahoo) to submit a term sheet. "If you are interested," I told them, "please put your best foot forward ASAP. Our train is leaving the station."

Google submitted an offer that was $100 million higher than Salesforce's. But we felt more comfortable with Marc and Salesforce and were concerned that federal regulators would hold up any deal with Google. So, after a quick negotiation, we agreed to terms the following week to sell to Salesforce.

Facebook went public on Friday, May 18. The stock fell 50 percent in early trading, giving Marc an easy excuse to renegotiate our deal or pull out altogether. But he had given us his word and stood by it. This was one of many situations where I witnessed Marc doing the hard right thing even when he could have made a different decision. We are forever grateful for how he acted under what must have been intense pressure from his board, which no doubt saw Facebook's IPO as even more proof that he was overpaying for Buddy Media.

Less than two weeks later, Eric Hippeau, the former CEO of Huffington Post who represented our investor Softbank Ventures on the Buddy Media board, forwarded me an email from famed tech reporter Kara Swisher.

"We have it on very good source that Buddy Media is about to sell to Salesforce," the email said. "I don't suppose we can talk off the record?"

We didn't respond to Kara but Peter Kafka broke the news later that day in *The Wall Street Journal*'s AllThingsD.

"Sources say the two companies have agreed to terms that will value Buddy Media at more than $800 million, but that the transaction hasn't closed yet," Pete reported. "People familiar with the deal say Buddy Media chose Salesforce's offer over a competitive bid from Google."[*]

The story broke as I was pulling into the publication's D: All Things Digital Conference at the Terranea resort in Rancho Palos Verdes, California, an annual event I attended that brings together the who's who of tech. We hadn't told our employees or clients about the deal, and I realized I shouldn't be pummeled by questions about the acquisition at a conference. I asked the driver to turn around and headed to the nearby house of my friends Renny and Erica Maslow in Beachwood Canyon to deal with the leak.

A few days later—Monday, June 4, 2012—I walked on stage to a thundering standing ovation in a Soho hotel ballroom full of Buddies. No one cheered louder than Kass, who sat in the front row

---

[*] Kafka, Peter. "Salesforce Set to Snap Up Facebook Friend Buddy Media for More Than $800 Million." *The Wall Street Journal*, May 29, 2012. https://allthingsd.com/20120529/salesforce-set-to-snap-up-facebook-friend-buddy-media-for-more-than-800-million/.

wearing a pink scarf and a smile that radiated pure joy. Her fist thrust triumphantly into the air. Her eyes sparkled with pride.*

For a few minutes that morning, the pressurized powder keg of our lives gave way to a euphoric explosion of emotional energy that is hard to describe. After eighteen years of shoveling together, sacrificing together, and parenting together, it all seemed worth it for one brief moment, even though our family was in shambles.

As we wrapped up for the day and headed uptown to meet our kids for dinner, we didn't discuss the money we would make or the opportunities the sale would provide. We didn't gloat or pat ourselves on the back for a job well done.

We spoke about how lucky we were to build companies and to do it together. We spoke about how thankful we were for all the people who supported us and believed in us. We discussed what we needed to do to heal our hurting family. We then spoke about who was going to take the kids to the doctor's office for their camp check-up the next day.

FOR THE LOVE OF BUILDING

As the cofounder who stood on stages and was featured in the press, I got most of the credit for our business successes. I was named the Ernst & Young Entrepreneur of the Year, not Kass. I was named Fortune Magazine's 40 Under 40, not Kass. But we knew the truth—Kass and I were, and are, equal partners. Neither of us would have been able to build Buddy Media alone.

---

* Lazerow, Michael. "This is the most amazing feeling I've ever had at work." *Facebook,* June 4, 2012. https://www.facebook.com/lazerow/videos/10151002915640289.

Part of my interest in writing this book was to document Kass's behind-the-scenes work that has created the life we have today. Most of the lessons came from her experience operating businesses. We still have a few years before she might have to change my adult diapers, but she's already spent years cleaning up the crap from my mistakes.

Some relationships are built on shared interests in a sport, a hobby, a musical genre, a religion, or a way of life. Ours is an almost-thirty-year love affair based on gritty hard work—building companies, our family, and our home, as well as countless memories and deep relationships with our close friends and colleagues.

We don't share all of the same interests or hobbies. I like live music and have been to too many Phish shows to count. Kass couldn't care less about live music shows, cares even less about Phish, and is now really into pickleball.

I (Kass) like to compete, play sports when I can, organize anything (physically and on spreadsheets!), be with my dogs, and watch stupid TV. Mike enjoys time with the dogs, but doesn't build his world around rows and columns and can always find an excuse to avoid mindless television.

Most couples share interests they pursue on the weekends. We share the love of daily shoveling. Shoveling with purpose. Building together all day, every day, is not for everyone. But it has been the gift of our lifetime. We can think of no better way to spend the days, weeks, months, years, and decades we have on earth.

We have met so many people we would never have met without taking the non-traditional path.

We have visited so many places we would never have seen if we had decided to sit behind a desk all day.

We have experienced emotions we never would have felt if we had played it safe.

We have taken gut-punching losses with businesses that failed, and we regret missed opportunities or misplaced priorities with our family. But we also have tasted what winning on the grandest stages is like.

While neither of us started companies solely to make money, the financial rewards have enabled us to do more of what matters to us.

It is true. Money doesn't buy happiness. But it does buy freedom and security, two things we cherish that are in short supply today.

The money has given us the freedom and security to continue our journey as entrepreneurs and investors. It has also allowed us to give back in ways we never thought possible. Marc Benioff once said that the best drug he ever took was philanthropy. "Nothing made me feel better," he said. "I highly recommend it."[*] We couldn't agree more.

If you want to impact the world, start a company and make a ton of money. Don't be ashamed of wanting to make money. Only be ashamed if you make your money and squander your opportunity to give back and make a difference.

For us, this has meant increasing our commitment to fighting rare cancers through Cycle for Survival. The movement is as strong as ever, and we are proud of our small part in its success and are donating 10 percent of the gross sales of this book to the cause.[†]

---

[*] Benioff, Marc. "The best drug I ever took was philanthropy. Nothing made me feel better. I highly recommend it." *Twitter,* July 12, 2013. https://twitter.com/Benioff/status/355716072588062721.

[†] To learn more, visit www.shovelingshit.com.

We have funded scholarships for Northwestern students attending the Medill Journalism School who otherwise would never have had the opportunity to get the type of education we received. And we are looking to take our giving to the next level as we learn more about accountable giving strategies while supporting our friends' causes along the way.

Thriving as an entrepreneur starts with learning to love the almighty shovel. Only those truly in love with shoveling will endure the crap needed to earn the money. And trust us. The crap doesn't shovel itself.

Each day brings new battles and new fights to keep the business alive, growing, and moving forward. It takes an unreasonable commitment that most people aren't willing to make. Shoveling shit is a thankless job—years of hard, unglamorous work unrecognized by others. Those who seek external validation should stay away. In this lonely struggle, true entrepreneurial spirit is forged with perseverance and resilience.

The immense pressure is not inherently good or bad. It just is.

If you decide to leap, you will be given the most precious gift of your life—purpose and fulfillment. But we hope that you heed our warning about the psychological scars—burnout, stress, and depression—and physical tolls, and find strategies that work for you to stay as mentally and physically fit and resilient as possible.

The act of creating, building, and growing puts you on a path that is difficult to find in a more traditional job setting. It is a path of personal growth and self-discovery. At the end of the path, there is the potential for financial gain, but more than that, there is a chance to create value for others and make an impact.

A MINDSET OF SHOVEL LOVE

The entrepreneurs who make it through the misery maze—those who reach profitability, sell their businesses for a profit, or take them public—all share a common mindset: the entrepreneur's mindset. It's a mindset of pure love—specifically, the love of hard work.

We have lived this mindset our entire lives, and only in hindsight can we recognize it, name it, and unpack it. It's a mindset that, in many ways, is unique to entrepreneurs—not better than anyone else's, but definitely different.

Entrepreneurs are not smarter. Walk into any college campus or corporation, law firm, ad agency, or consultancy, and you will quickly bump into smart people who will never start a business.

Entrepreneurs are not more talented. Every high-performing organization has talented people.

Entrepreneurs are not more strategic. Business schools manufacture strategic thinkers and many will never start a company.

Entrepreneurs are not more committed to hard work. Every successful leader puts in long hours and shovels tons of crap.

What makes entrepreneurs different is that they shovel like crazy when there's nothing to their business but a vision and a plan written on a napkin—and they love doing it. The relationship with hard work from a pit of deep uncertainty lives in the heart, not the head. It's full of passion, commitment, and joy. It is unconditional and transcends a mere occupational commitment.

It has never been a burden we bear but a beloved endeavor we share with each other and all the founders we have met on our journey. That doesn't mean we have liked everything about it. Our hard work has produced enough pain for us and our kids to fill its own book. Like any great relationship, it has not always been easy, but has always been worth the fight.

Just like romantic love has been harnessed by artists for thousands of years to produce countless plays, songs, movies, paintings, and other works of beauty, the love between entrepreneurs and shoveling shit has produced the world's greatest companies and millions of others that are less well-known but no less beloved by their founders.

No group understands the J. Cole rap lyric (that our son Myles also has tattooed on his arm) better than entrepreneurs, "It's beauty in the struggle, ugliness in the success."[*]

It's inside their struggles that entrepreneurs often find their reward—the purpose and passion to keep going despite the circumstances. The entrepreneur's mindset recognizes virtue in shoveling in complete darkness. It's a mindset that is unique to and inseparable from them.

And that's why we consider our entrepreneurial life—and this book—a love story.

A love story that is unique to us and shared by us. And a love story that is universal—shared by every man and woman with the courage to start shoveling despite the low odds and uncertain ending.

Our love is the story of finding peace that goes beyond any traditional financial measure of success. Shoveling together was not just a worthwhile endeavor but a remarkable way to build our love and respect for each other and an extraordinarily meaningful shared existence.

---

[*] J. Cole. "*Love Yourz.*" Track 11 on *2014 Forest Hills Drive*. Roc Nation, 2014.

Shoveling shit is not for everyone. But if you decide it's for you, grab a shovel and start a business. Because entrepreneurs who love to shovel are unstoppable!

ACKNOWLEDGMENTS

Everything worthwhile that we have done has been hard, and writing this book was no exception. However, one of the great benefits was reliving so many memories, which evoked tremendous gratitude for the hundreds of people who supported Team Lazerow over the past fifty years. None of what is in this book would have been possible without a long list of family, mentors, colleagues, and friends.

Our parents' love, life lessons, advice, and resources shaped us. Ralph, Sheila (RIP), Nancy, Harold, Arthur and Tina were there for us no matter the situation, and we are thankful for their unconditional support.

Much of our ability to work within a group stems from our roles as the youngest (Kass) and middle (Mike) children. So our siblings—Andrew, Leslie, John, Robert, Juleen, Ralph, and James—played an essential part in our story. And when we talk about siblings, we have to include my (Kass's) beloved "fruzin"

Julia, my sister from my other mother (beloved Aunt Boo). She is more than a cousin and sister to me, she is a deeply loyal friend I turn to when I need someone.

This book and our life together would have never existed without Kevin and Jill Kane, and we are thankful to them and their Allentown, Pennsylvania, wedding, which was ground zero for our relationship.

While we were not always present for our kids when they were growing up, we had a team of babysitters who served as our proxy. We could never have raised such amazing people without all of them. A special thanks to Jessica Erazo, Stephanie Surti, and Jen Brissman.

We're also thankful to early mentors like Mary Dedinsky and Diane Hartley. As my (Mike's) college advisor, Mary pushed me to start on my path as a young entrepreneur when I walked into her office with an idea for an internet business. She propped me up when I needed it, believing in me before I believed in myself. And Diane Hartley has been my (Kass's) guiding light. I think of her often and have carried all that she taught me into every company and parental decision I have made.

Our first cofounder and friend, Mike Caspar, and his brilliant wife, Elena, brought technical abilities and a get-it-done attitude that perfectly complemented our strengths. Launching an internet business in 1998 was not easy. No-code platforms and cloud software for product launches didn't exist. We could never have done it without them.

There is not enough gratitude in the universe to express how thankful we are to Buddy Media cofounder Jeff Ragovin. He shovels harder than anyone we know, his zest for life is contagious, and

Acknowledgments

his generosity knows no bounds. We are lucky to be best friends and family with Jeff and Kurt Giehl.

Katherine Bateman's dive-in-and-roll-up-your-sleeves, always-on work ethic and brilliant brand marketing mind shaped the Golf.com and Buddy Media brands and every brand we have touched since. She has always been more than just an amazing partner in our businesses; she's a loyal, unconditional friend and a trusted support system to our family.

Jeff Berman's operational advice and unconditional support were game-changers as we grew. His friendship, character, belief in doing what is right at all times, and humor continue to enrich our lives on a daily basis.

Several non-relative investors in Golf.com and Buddy Media trusted us and provided the fuel to keep us going before we were known quantities—Jim Manuel, Al Taubman, Mason Myers, Andrew and Sam Kartalis, Jeremy Mindich, Matt Sirovich, Richard Hochman, Catherine Levene and the New York Times digital team, Fred Wynne, Matthias Lydon, Steven Miller, Stuart Sundlun, Larry Oberman, John and Alison Puth, Dr. Richard and Lori Rabinowitz, Steven Reitman, Donald and Nancy Surber, Jay Weitzman, Robert and Cynthia Zender, Greg Stuart, Peter Thiel, Salil Deshpande, Mark Pincus, Kenny Finklestein, Brian Bedol, James Altucher, Byron Denenberg, Eric Hippeau, Jordy Levy, Mark Read, Sheila Spence, Sir Martin Sorrell and the WPP team, Ron Conway, Jules Maltz and the IVP team, Jeff Richards, Glenn Solomon and the Notable Capital team, and Deven Parekh and the Insight team.

And we owe a special thanks to a few investors whose guidance and friendship transcended all definitions of the investor-entrepreneur bond.

Keith Bank committed to investing in Golf.com and helped us find additional investors who kept us going when it looked like we were on a sinking ship. Alan Patricof, Ian Sigalow, and Dana Settle, who trusted us, made Buddy Media one of Greycroft's early portfolio companies and never stopped working tirelessly on our behalf. Karin Klein fought for us at Softbank and continues to root for us. Roger Ehrenberg's introductions to series A investors paved the way for Buddy Media's most important financing. And Howard Lindzon was the first investor to commit to Buddy Media and shoveled alongside us. Life wouldn't be the same without these great friends and supporters.

Words cannot express our gratitude for the hundreds of Buddy Media employees and advisers who also shoveled with us. While we can't list them all, we feel compelled to recognize a few.

Abby Lauterbach's infectious enthusiasm, team focus, and wide-ranging skillsets not only helped launch Buddy Media on both coasts, but also helped create and maintain the Buddy Media culture throughout the five years.

Michael Jaindl (MJ)'s integrity, commitment, and dependability shined through from the beginning and also paved the way for our massive client relationship success.

Patrick Stokes brought a get-it-done attitude to architecting and executing our product roadmap even when we set unreasonable deadlines and pivoted (sometimes without telling him, like when Mike announced a new product we hadn't even started to build!).

Brittany White's attention to details that mattered, dedication, loyalty, and amazing sense of humor helped us build, scale, and sell our company.

Pam Schloss' unwavering positivity and exceptional understanding of the Buddy Media culture were instrumental in hiring and creating the team we needed to succeed.

Natalie Stein's can-do, deal-maker attitude as our general counsel served as a competitive weapon, allowing us to move quickly and aggressively without breaking anything we couldn't easily glue back together.

Joe Ciarallo's deep knowledge and connections put me (Mike) on more stages and in more publications than any startup CEO deserves.

Michael Kassan's support and advice helped us close many of our most significant deals and partnerships, and he continues to serve as our confidante.

And Gary Vaynerchuk, whose support of this book is just the latest example of his friendship, partnership, and advice over the past fifteen years. Gary has helped us dream even bigger and shovel even harder. He pushed us to tell our story, and we are grateful he did.

No entrepreneur can do what they do without a team of professionals behind them. And ours has been the best of the best. Ethan Skerry, now at Fenwick, did an amazing job representing Time Inc. in the Golf.com transaction. So great, in fact, that we asked you to represent us early on at Buddy Media. He thankfully agreed and laid the legal foundation for our growth. Lowenstein Sandler's tech head Ed Zimmerman provided impactful legal support—and epic wine—during our most critical times and continues to be one of our most important advocates and allies.

A special thanks to Claire Mildren for jumping in and making such a big impact so quickly.

Lastly, we extend our deepest gratitude to Team *Shoveling $h!t*! This journey would not have been possible without the invaluable help and guidance of Stephen Caldwell. We are also profoundly thankful to Paul Grignon for his outstanding work on the cover and for always helping us when we need him. Special thanks to Kristen Hughes and Jen Jaxan for their instrumental efforts in helping us bring our content to life. And a heartfelt thanks to Naren Aryal, Will Wolfslau, Lauren Magnussen, and the entire team at Amplify Publishing, along with the Brand Building Group team, for their dedication in helping us launch a book that truly captures the beauty and challenges of the entrepreneurial journey.

ABOUT THE AUTHORS

Mike and Kass Lazerow are serial entrepreneurs and investors best known as the cofounders of Golf.com and Buddy Media, a software company that sold to Salesforce.com for $745 million.

With a lifetime of stories from decades of building businesses and helping others as investors and advisors, they are in high demand as public speakers, writers, and podcast guests.

Their journey began as friends growing up in the suburbs of the nation's capital. They started dating after reuniting at a mutual friend's wedding in 1996. Two years later, they did what all new couples deeply in love do—cofounded a company, Golf.com, before marrying in 1999.

After selling Golf.com to Time Warner in 2006, Mike and Kass cofounded Buddy Media, which would become the world's leading social media marketing platform. And since selling Buddy Media to Salesforce in 2012, they have focused on providing capital and advice to the world's most innovative founders.

Mike and Kass have supported close to 100 early-stage startup founders. They served as angel investors and advisors to Scopely, which sold to Savvy Games for $5 billion in 2022, and Liquid Death, the canned water company whose "evil mission" is to make people laugh and get more of them to drink healthy beverages more often, all while helping to kill plastic pollution.

Mike was named New York's Ernst & Young Entrepreneur Of The Year®, and together they were ranked number one on *Business Insider*'s Silicon Alley 100, received the Cycle for Survival Game Changer Award for their leadership in helping to raise $375 million for cancer research, and were recognized with the Leader of the Future Award from the Frances Hesselbein Leadership Institute.

Mike and Kass live in New York City and the Hudson Valley and have three grown children (Myles, Cole, and Vivian) and two rescue dogs (Cece and Gizmo).